MODERN BATTLE TANKS

Edited by Duncan Crow

Published by
ARCO PUBLISHING COMPANY, INC.
New York

Published 1978 by Arco Publishing Company, Inc.
219 Park Avenue South, New York, N.Y. 10003

Copyright © 1978 PROFILE PUBLICATIONS LIMITED.

Library of Congress Cataloging in Publication Data

MODERN BATTLE TANKS

1. Tanks (Military science) I. Crow, Duncan.
UG446.5.M55   358'.18   78-4192
ISBN 0-668-04650-3 pbk

Printed in Spain by Heraclio Fournier, S.A.
Vitoria Spain

Contents

S-Tank

by R. M. Ogorkiewicz

AMX 30 Battle Tank

by R. M. Ogorkiewicz

Coloured illustrations by Tom Brittain, Terry Hadler, Martin Lee and Mike Trim

Introduction

Many armoured vehicles today are referred to as tanks which do not properly warrant the name. As far as most newspaper readers and television viewers are concerned any vehicle that is armed and armoured is a tank whether it has tracks or wheels. And indeed in some cases a definition is hard to frame. But there is one class of armoured vehicle about which there can be no question as to whether it is a tank or not – the Main Battle Tank. The term first came into use in the 1950s and has replaced such classifications as medium, cruiser, and heavy and medium gun tanks.

The function of a modern battle tank is to strike the enemy from a distance and to be able to close with the target while at the same time being to a considerable degree protected.

Nine countries manufacture main battle tanks today: France (AMX 30), Germany (Leopard), Great Britain (Chieftain), India (Vijayanta, Vickers Battle Tank), Japan (Type 61), the Soviet Union (T62 and T72), Sweden (S-Tank Strv 103), Switzerland (Pz 61 and 68), and the United States (M60 series). As well as these there are earlier generation MBTs still in use in a number of armies: the British-built Centurion, the Russian T54 and T55, and the American M47 and M48 (the M47 being now almost completely phased out).

The AMX 30, Leopard, Chieftain, Vickers, T62 and M60 have all been exported and are in service in armies other than their native ones, as are all the earlier generation MBTs listed above. As an example of overseas sales the Russian T54-55s may be cited. It is estimated that to the end of 1975 the Russians had sold some 15,000 of these tanks around the world from Vietnam to the Middle East. Two countries, China and Israel, may also be building their own MBTs which they have designed themselves, but are more likely to be simply developing and adapting imported or acquired vehicles.

This book contains Profiles of eight of the most important MBTs in service today. The other current MBTs are the Japanese Type 61 and its successor, the Swiss Pz 61 and 68, the Vickers (Vijayanta) and that most durable of MBTs (so long in service indeed that it was first built before the term came into existence and has in its own existence spanned more than half the history of the tank): the Centurion.

The Centurion

After World War II the British found themselves the only European producers of a modern battle tank. With no other country in the West other than the Americans having the capabilities at that time of producing a new tank, Britain sold some 3,000 Centurions to other countries during the 1950s, in addition to the 1,500 required for the British army.

The Centurion was originally designed in 1943 to fight the increasingly powerful tanks that the Germans were producing. In May 1945 the first six prototypes available were rushed to the British 22nd Armoured Brigade of the 7th Armoured Division in Germany but they arrived just too late to see action. These six were part of an order for 20. Next in production came the Centurion 1 of which there were 100, and Centurion 2 – another 100. In the end Centurion appeared in 21 versions, 13 of which were gun tanks.

Centurion 2 was up-armoured and had a new design of turret of cast armour, Centurion 1's turret being fabricated. Later Centurion 2s had the new 20-pounder gun instead of the 17-pounder and these were designated Centurion 3. Most Mark 2s were converted to Mark 3s in 1950–51 and some subsequently to Mark 5. It was the Centurion 3 that first saw action. In the hands of the 8th King's Royal Irish Hussars (now part of The Queen's Royal Irish Hussars) Centurions began their long and trustworthy fighting career on 3 January 1951 in Korea.

Centurion 4 would have been equipped with the 95mm howitzer for close support role, but in 1949 this proposal was dropped. Late in 1952 Centurion 5 appeared under the design parentage of Vickers-Armstrongs Ltd. Basically it was the Mark 3 with the co-axial Besa replaced by a .30 inch Browning. It had a driver's compartment with ammunition stowage, a fighting compartment for the rest of the crew in the centre of the hull, and two rear compartments for the engine and transmission components. The power-operated turret contained the 20-pounder gun, the co-axial Browning, more ammunition and the radio equipment. The armament was supported and protected by the rectangular external mantlet. To avoid damage whilst moving the gun could be clamped internally or secured in a travelling crutch. The sight mounting permitted direct, semi-direct or completely indirect fire.

The driver's compartment was reached either from the double hatches in the hull roof or from the turret. Clutch, brake and accelerator controls were conventionally arranged. The Meteor 4B engine was a development of the Rolls-Royce Merlin aircraft engine which had been installed in the Comet and Cromwell tanks. It had two banks of 6 cylinders and by the use of spring-loaded governors the engine revs were limited to 2,550 rpm. As well as the main generator there was an auxiliary self-contained charging set to meet the extra requirements of a fighting load. There were two internal fuel tanks and a Kigass priming system for extra cold starting.

The traversely mounted Merritt-Brown gearbox had five forward and two reverse speeds. The final drive had double reduction gear trains. The turning circle depended upon the gear selected, therefore a driver needed practice to become proficient.

There were three suspension units on each side and the front and rear units had four hydraulic shock absorbers; all units were supported on two pairs of rubber road wheels. This modified Horstmann suspension was also used on the Conqueror Heavy Gun Tank and later on the Chieftain. Side plates were fitted to provide protection for the suspension and for the hull sides.

Subsequent Centurion development was:

Mark 7: increased fuel capacity by addition of internal tank at rear of transmission compartment. Improved ammunition stowage including side loading hatch on left hull side. Large headlights. Appeared in late 1952. Design parents were Leyland Motors.

Mark 8: As for Mark 7. Resiliently mounted gun mantlet (no canvas cover). Commander's cupola doors in two parts – enabling "umbrella" position for better observation. Cupola counter-rotates to assist in target acquisition. Changes in gun control equipment.

Marks 5/1, 7/1 and 8/1: As for original Marks but up-armoured. A retrospective modification.

Marks 5/2, 7/2 and 8/2: As for original Marks but with 105mm gun and new ammunition stowage. Barrel similar to 20-pounder Type B but with fume extractor mounted eccentrically. A retrospective modification.

Marks 6, 9 and 10: Marks 5, 7 and 8 respectively that incorporated both up-gunning and up-armouring modifications. Mark 6 normally had an armoured fuel tank mounted on rear of hull adding 38 inches to length.

Marks 6/1, 9/1 and 10/1: Marks 6, 9 and 10 fitted with infra-red night fighting equipment. Searchlight on turret, stowage basket on turret rear. IR driving lights.

Marks 6/2, 9/2 and 10/2: Marks 6, 9 and 10 with coaxially-mounted ranging gun.

Marks 11, 12 and 13: Marks 6, 9 and 10 respectively which incorporated both night fighting and ranging gun modifications.

The leading characteristics of Centurion 13, last of the line, are:

Engine, make	Meteor 4B
horse power	650
Fuel capacity	1,040 litres
Range, roads	185 km
Armour	152mm max, 76mm min
Weight, unloaded	49,800 kg
combat loaded	51,800 kg
Power to weight ratio	12.2
Ground pressure	0.94 kg/cm²
Length with gun forward	9.82 m
with gun in travelling lock	7.82 m
Width without skirts	3.30 m
with skirts	3.40 m
Height overall	2.96 m
Ground clearance	0.51 m
Maximum road speed	35 km/hr
Gun, calibre	105mm
length	51 calibres
ammunition	70 rounds
Coaxial gun	7.62mm L8A1
Machine-gun, external	7.62mm L37A1
Machine-gun, ranging, coaxial	12.7mm L21A1
Crew	4

Swiss Pz 61 and Pz 68

Among the many countries which bought Centurions was Switzerland. The Swiss read the lesson of the Korean War that tanks were still effective and that the best defence against them was other tanks. They bought 200 AMX13s from France and 300 Centurions from Britain and South Africa. Meanwhile they embarked on building their own tank.

The first tank to be built by the Swiss was the Pz 58. The idea was proposed in 1951 and the first prototype was completed in 1958 by the Federal Construction Works at Thun. It was armed with a modified version of the Swiss 90mm anti-tank gun. The second prototype, completed the following year, was armed with the British 20-pounder. In 1961 it was decided to adopt the new British 105mm gun and this up-gunned version of the Pz 58 was designated the Pz 61.

Between 1964 and 1966 the Swiss built 150 Pz 61s. These tanks are light in weight – 38,000 kg – making them virtually the same in mass as the Vijayanta and the Japanese STB. They are also narrow – 3.06 m; narrower indeed than any other contemporary battle tank. This narrowness was achieved by the integration of the gun ammunition with the fuel tanks at the front of the hull on either side of the driver.

The hull was cast in one piece, as was also the turret which dispensed with the rear bulge usual in tanks since World War II. There were two cupolas, one fitted with eight episcopes for the commander, the other with six vision blocks for the loader. The 105mm gun, a modified version of the British L7A1, was mounted in the turret and fired APDS projectiles, HESH ammunition and Swiss-made HE rounds. The modification was a Swiss-made breech block of the horizontal type. There was an optical range-finder operated by the commander. A 20mm Oerlikon gun was mounted alongside the main armament and a 7.5mm MG51 machine gun was mounted on the top of the commander's cupola. The gun elevation and turret traverse were operated by an electro-hydraulic system made in France. Apart from this the only major component of the Pz 61 not manufactured in Switzerland was its engine, which was made in Stuttgart by Daimler-Benz AG and is very similar to the German Leopard's engine except that it is a V-8 instead of a V-10. The Pz 61's engine was in fact adopted earlier so that the Leopard's engine could benefit from experience gained with the Pz 61 prototypes.

The transmission system is the product of SLM of Winterthur consisting of a multi-clutch semi-automatic gearbox with 6 forward and 2 reverse speeds and a double differential steering system with a hydrostatic steering drive. As R. M. Ogorkiewicz has written in a Profile of Swiss Battle Tanks, "the Pz 61 was only the second tank ever to be built with such a sophisticated steering system – the first being the French Char B of the thirties – which gives it infinitely variable control over the turning radius and in the writer's experience makes it one of the most pleasant tanks to steer. . . . Another interesting design feature of the Pz 61 is its suspension. This includes six road wheels on each side which are all independently located and sprung by means of stacks of Belleville washers, or conical springs. The use of this form of springing was first proposed in Germany towards the end of World War II for tanks of the E-series which were then being designed, because of the large amount of energy it could absorb in relation to its size and weight. However, the Pz 61 was the first tank to be built with such springing." Belleville washers can be installed outside the hull. As a result a valuable amount of space was saved within the Pz 61's armour envelope.

The Pz 68 was ordered in 1968 and delivery started in 1971. The most important difference from the Pz 61 was the addition of a hydro-electric stabilisation system to maintain the gun in position whilst the tank was in motion. The secondary armament was changed from a 20mm Oerlikon to a 7.5mm MG 51. The engine was also uprated to produce 660 bhp thus increasing maximum road speed to 60 kmh. The original all-steel dry-pin track was replaced by a slightly wider track with rubber bushed pins and rubber road pads.

The Pz 61 has served as the basis for an armoured recovery vehicle, an armoured bridgelayer, and a self-propelled gun. Its leading characteristics are:

Gun, calibre	105mm
length	51 calibres
ammunition	52 rounds
Coaxial gun	20mm Oerlikon
Machine-gun, external	7.5mm MG 51
Weight, net	37,000 kg
combat loaded	38,000 kg
Length, overall, with gun forward	9.36 m
overall, without gun	6.685 m
Width, overall	3.06 m
Height, to turret roof	2.47 m
to top of loader's cupola	2.72 m
Ground clearance	0.42 m
Width of tracks	0.50 m
Track length to centre distance ratio	1.66 : 1
Ground pressure	0.85 kg/cm^2
Engine, type	V-8 diesel
make	Daimler Benz
model	MB 837
gross horse power	630
Maximum road speed	55 km/hr
Range, roads	300 km
Crew	4

Vickers Battle Tank

While they were working on the Centurion and the Chieftain for the British Army Vickers-Armstrongs Ltd. also designed a battle tank on their own initiative. Weighing 38 tonnes or 37½ English tons laden, (hence its familiar name the Vickers 37 ton tank), its layout is conventional with the driver's compartment and ammunition stowage in the forward part of its hull, the fighting compartment, surmounted by the turret carrying the main and secondary armament, in the centre, and the engine and transmission compartment in the rear. The hull itself is welded from homogeneous rolled steel armour plates which provide a reasonable degree of protection for the crew and the components located in it, and although, as R. M. Ogorkiewicz has pointed out, the protection is "inevitably inferior to that of the much heavier Chieftain it is very similar to that of other tanks of its weight, except for Russian tanks, which have thicker armour but at the cost of cramped crew compartments. The Vickers tank, on the other hand, has a relatively roomy hull to enable its four-man crew to operate it more efficiently, particularly under tropical or semi-tropical conditions."

The turret too is welded from homogeneous rolled steel plates. This made it unique until the appearance of the US-German MBT-70 experimental tank, first built in prototype form in 1967, and the more recent Leopard 2 whose turrets have been fabricated from rolled plates.

"Apart from the stabilisation of the gunner's sight, the ability of the crew to observe and to detect targets when the tank is moving off the road, especially when it is "buttoned up", depends to a very large extent on the quality of the ride it provides and, therefore on its suspension. This consists of six double, rubber-tyred road wheels on each side which are mounted on trailing arms and independently sprung by transversely located torsion bars. To prevent corrosion and to protect their highly stressed skins from being scratched, the twelve hull-mounted torsion bars are wrapped. In addition there are also short torsion bars within the first, second and last trailing arms on each side which are brought into action when the arms approach the bump position, by stops fixed to the hull. This most unusual spring arrangement approaches the ideal of a spring rate which increases the wheel movement and thereby improves the ride of the tank. In addition to their secondary torsion bars, the first, second and last road wheel stations on each side are fitted with hydraulic dampers."

Drive from the Leyland L60 water-cooled diesel engine is taken through a centrifugal clutch to a TN12 transmission which was originally produced for the Chieftain. The gearbox provides six forward and two reverse speeds. There is also an auxiliary engine, as in the Chieftain, to drive a second 24-volt generator when the main engine is not running. The tank can be fitted with a collapsible flotation screen which enables it to swim across water obstacles too deep for fording.

The Mark 1 version of the Vickers was adopted by the Indian Army as its main battle tank and put into production in 1964, and was delivered to them in 1965. The following year, a factory which had been built at Avadi near Madras, began producing tanks, the first ever on the Indian sub-continent. The Indian army named it the Vijayanta which is Sanskrit for "Conqueror". Kuwait also ordered the tank which was essentially the same as the Mark 1 developed for India. The first tank was delivered to Kuwait in January 1971.

Development has continued. The Mark 2 was a Mark 1 modified to carry four Swingfire anti-tank guided missiles in addition to its usual gun armament. There is also a Mark 3 which differs from the Mark 1, "mainly in having a turret with a well-shaped cast front welded to a fabricated armour plate body. It also

has a cast gun mantlet which is better shaped from the point of view of its resistance to armour-piercing projectiles than the flat mantlet of the Mark 1. The front glacis plate is also a casting which improves its ballistic shape. In addition the Mark 3 embodies various other improvements, such as an increase in the depression of its gun from 7 to 10 degrees below the horizontal and an increase in the ammunition stowage to 50 rounds.

"Otherwise the Mark 3 version retains the basic characteristics of the Vickers battle tank, which is uncomplicated and robust. At the same time it offers a combination of highly effective armament with a high degree of mobility at a cost which compares favourably with that of other contemporary battle tanks."

The leading characteristics of the Vickers battle tank Mark 1 are:

Gun, calibre	105mm
length	51 calibres
ammunition	44 rounds
Machine-gun, ranging	12.7mm
coaxial	0.30in
external	0.30in
Weight, unladen	36,000 kg
laden	38,100 kg
Length, overall, gun forward	9.73 m
vehicle only	7.29 m
Height, to turret roof	2.44 m
to top of periscopes	2.64 m
Width, overall	3.17 m
Ground clearance	0.41 m
Width of tracks	0.52 m
Nominal ground pressure	0.9 kg/cm^2
Engine, make and model	Leyland L60
gross horsepower	600
Maximum road speed	48 km/hr
Range, on roads	600 km
Crew	4

Japanese Type 61 and STB

(Based on information kindly given to the editor by Lieutenant-General Tomio Hara, I.J.A., Retd.)

In 1954 Japan, which had been one of the leading tank manufacturing countries until 1945, began work on a development programme for a new battle tank, the Type 61 as it was to become. The designers and main contractors were Mitsubishi Heavy Industries.

The new tank was to have a similar or better performance than that of current U.S. medium tanks. As main armament the 90mm gun was chosen because at that time it was being used by other countries as the standard tank gun and because of its high reputation. Weight was limited to 35 tons for railway transportation reasons, which also limited the width to 3 metres. This design handicap was overcome by economising on the size of the fighting compartment and minimising the silhouette without cutting down on the protective armour. Speed was to be 45 km/hr, which was slower than other comparable tanks. An existing diesel engine was to be used.

Two prototypes, STA-1 and STA-2, were completed by March 1957. After evaluation two more prototypes, STA-3 and STA-4, were built. They were completed in 1960 and were given the official title of the Type 61 Tank with Type 61 90mm Tank Gun the following year. Production began in 1962. A bridging tank and a recovery tank were also built using the Type 61 chassis. Type 61 tanks gradually replaced the American M4 Medium in Japanese service.

Research work was now begun on a further main battle tank to keep pace with developments in other countries: the U.S. M60, the West German Leopard, the French AMX 30, and the U.S.-West German MBT 70. The most significant change in modern tanks was the increase in tank gun calibre from 90mm to 105mm. Furthermore, with improved fire control systems the range of the gun could be increased; this meant that ammunition needed to have a greater penetrating ability. The Japanese therefore decided that in spite of railway transportation limitations they needed a tank which could be equipped with a 105mm gun and would have an improved rate of fire, greater first round accuracy, and an electronic fire-control system.

Research was carried out on suspension systems to provide improved mobility, especially in paddy fields. The new tank was to be about ten per cent heavier than the Type 61 because the armour would be thickened to give more protection. Weight would be about 38 tons.

Construction of the first two STB prototypes started in 1968 and finished in September 1969. Special efforts were made to lower the height of the vehicle and thus make the silhouette as low as possible. By using a hydro-pneumatic suspension system the vehicle's height was adjustable. Hull slope and shape were designed to give maximum protection.

Despite the height and width limitations a 105mm gun was successfully mounted without causing hindrance to combat movements. A semi-automatic feed system was used to increase the rate of fire, with the rounds being brought up to the breech by an electrically-operated chain and then loaded manually into the chamber. A dual axis gyro was used to assist rapid sighting and the balancing of the barrel yaw and pitch. A laser range-finder was adopted and there was a ballistic electronic computer for the gun.

Two more prototypes were built in 1970 and production of the new MBT was scheduled for 1974. The tank is equipped with a snorkel device and the hull is completely sealed for defence against CBR. There is an infra-red sight.

The leading characteristics of the Type 61 Tank are:

Armament, Gun		Type 61 90mm Tank Gun (in revolving turret)
	Coaxial machine-gun	0.30 calibre (in revolving turret)
	Machine-gun	0.50 (mounted on top of revolving machine-gun turret with sighting and firing operations from within machine-gun turret)
Crew		4 men
Combat Weight		35 tons
Transmission		Constant-mesh gear system with 5-speed forward and 1-speed reverse and addition of 2-speed exclusive high/low speed clutch controlled differential
Steering mechanism		controlled differential
Suspension system		torsion bar with shock absorber
Gun sighting		hydraulic and manual elevation and traverse
Engine		Mitsubishi 12HM21WT 4-cycle air-cooled 90 degree V12-cylinder turbocharged diesel with output of 570hp/2,100rpm.
Rangefinder		located within the machine-gun turret with 1.0m datum line and coincidence type.
Overall length with gun		8.19 m
Hull length		6.30 m
Width		2.95 m
Height (top of gun turret)		2.49 m
Road clearance		0.40 m
Track width		0.50 m
Ground pressure		0.95 kg/cm^2
Maximum speed		45 km/hr

The specification of the STB tank first prototypes is:

Crew		4
Weight		38 tons
Dimensions		
	Length overall with gun	9.19 m
	Length overall chassis	6.60 m
	Width overall	3.18 m
	Height overall (top of turret)	2.25 m
	Ground clearance	0.40 m (adjustment range of plus 230mm minus 220mm)
	Ground contact length	4.00 m
	Track width	550mm
	Ground pressure	0.86 kg/cm^2
Engine		Mitsubishi 10ZF21WT 2-cycle air-cooled 90-degree V 10-cylinder multifuel engine with turbo-supercharger; bore 135mm; stroke 150mm; 720hp/2200rpm
Transmission-steering unit		
	Transmission	Powershift with 6 forward and 1 reverse speeds
	Steering	Epicyclic double differential type
	Suspension system	Hydro-pneumatic with height and posture changing capability.
Rear sprocket drive		
Armour: Hull		Rolled steel
	Turret	Cast steel
Maximum speed		50kmh

A group of T-62 tanks during the occupation of Prague in 1968. The changes in configuration of the turret are clearly visible. The white stripes on turret and hull identified all vehicles involved in the invasion force. (Photo: dpa)

Soviet Mediums T44, T54, T55 & T62

THE capitulation of the Third Reich and the occupation of Eastern Europe in the spring of 1945 offered an opportunity which the Russians were not slow to grasp. Three times they had been invaded from the west, twice within living memory by Germany, and one of the few factors that had saved them from subjugation each time was the sheer size of the country, although material losses were enormous and the political structure severely shaken. Expansion westward over the centuries had failed to find secure frontiers, but this time there seemed a real, if fortuitous, chance of establishing the next best thing; a glacis of subservient states to buffer the U.S.S.R. against the West, and especially against Germany.

This glacis had to be secured, both against the reluctance of Eastern Europe to be steered towards Communism and against the early predominance of the U.S.A. in nuclear weapons, and strong occupation forces were clearly seen to be necessary. As the Western powers had demobilised much more quickly meantime, these forces were in turn regarded as a direct threat to the security of Western Europe and the two opposing treaty organizations quickly followed one another into being. The present status quo had been reached.

Armoured forces had been largely instrumental in obtaining victory on the Eastern Front, but although there were some notable instances of the blitzkrieg technique being turned against its originators, much of the advance was dourly contested throughout. The

swiftest campaign, in fact, was conducted in Manchuria in August 1945 where 6th Guards Tank Army advanced 510 miles in 10 days, although against very light opposition. An interesting feature of this whirlwind manoeuvre was the use of airborne troops to seize objectives ahead of the ground troops as well as supply from the air, and both these methods have been emphasised in post-war tactics as being particularly relevant to any future war in Europe.

The most numerous type of tank at this time was the T-34, which was developed from Christie's T3 model in the U.S.A., through the BT series, A-20, A-30 and T-32, to the T-34/76 introduced in 1940. The later changes to the T-34 involved the installation of a three-man turret, mounting an 85-mm. gun of roughly equivalent performance to the early German 88-mm., on a hull whose power plant, transmission and running gear had been brought to a high state of reliability. In no other contemporary tank had firepower, mobility and protection been so well balanced. This excellence had not been achieved by any revolutionary steps in technology; indeed the upheavals in the Soviet armament industry due to the wholesale removal of most of it eastwards would have precluded these anyway. It was due more to a fine judgement on what were the essentials for a fighting vehicle, and the need to use resources in the most economical way.

What are the parameters that the post-war tank designer in the U.S.S.R. has to consider now? Firstly, the sheer size of the area and climatic conditions

1

The T-44 showing the driver's vision slit in the glacis plate, tracks, and the frontal aspect of the turret strongly reminiscent of the T-34/85.

The Russian tank-crewman is probably an adequate technician and civilian life has taught him to be adept at improvisation, but draconian discipline may often be necessary to overcome his natural distaste for routine or sustained exertion. He is taught that "the aggressive imperialist governments will attempt to unleash a future war . . . without warning, by means of a surprise attack"[1]. This must be countered by the use of nuclear and chemical strikes, followed by "mobile shock units operating . . . at lightning speed with rapid sorties penetrating the enemy positions to a considerable depth"[2], a doctrine which probably owes much to the influence of Frunze in the twenties who argued that the correct Marxist response to an attack was a swift and massive counter-stroke. These then are the conditions under which the Soviet tank must operate, some of them quite different to those to be considered by the designer in the West. The tactical doctrine itself highlights further differences and these will be returned to later.

involved, from the permanently frozen tundra in the Arctic Circle, through marshlands, steppes and deserts to the high mountains in the south-east. Equipment must also be able to operate in extremes of temperature as wide as $+40°$ to $-70°$ centigrade. Apart from the distances, roads are relatively few and far between except in Central Europe itself and although economics dictate that movement should be by rail wherever possible (thus imposing severe dimensional limitations on a tank design), long distances may have to be driven on indifferent surfaces where repair and supply facilities are likely to be almost non-existent. Moreover advances across Russia and Central Europe in an east-westerly direction will invariably involve the crossing of some large waterways and a host of minor ones. As the civilian communication networks are relatively undeveloped tactical flexibility demands a self-sufficiency in crossing these obstacles even without the risk of enemy action.

T-44

The first new Soviet medium tank to be seen after the war was the T-44 although production had probably started in 1944. It was similar in many ways to the T-34 but the thickness of the glacis plate had been increased to compensate for its being at a steeper angle, the hull gunner had been displaced altogether (as he already had been in the heavy tanks) leaving a Degtyarev (DT) 7·62-mm. MG mounted rigidly alongside the driver and firing through an aperture in the glacis plate. The driver's hatch was moved to the hull roof and he had only a narrow vision slit in the glacis itself. The sides of the hull were now vertical and thicker in order to accommodate the wider traverse ring for a turret whose sides were at a greater obliquity than was the case with the T-34/85. The 85-mm. gun was unchanged, however, although two more rounds were carried and the space vacated by the hull gunner

[1]Marshal V. D. Sokolovsky (Ed.), *Military Strategy*, Pall Mall, London 1963, p. 273.
[2]Ibid, p. 292.

The first version of the T-54 having an oval turret with a distinctive cut-away shape at the rear. (Photo: Lehmanns Verlag)

A platoon of the first version of the T-54 tank to be produced in quantity on exercise manned by the Soviet Taman Guards. The design of the turret has been altered but the early 100-mm. gun, with its plain section barrel without a fume extractor, has been retained.
(Photo: Camera Press)

may have been used to stow ammunition or to accommodate extra fuel tanks. The V-2 diesel engine may have been mounted transversely or tilted as the overall height of the vehicle was reduced by between 4 and 10 inches. The running gear appeared to be unchanged although there was now a wider gap between the 1st and 2nd pairs of road wheels instead of the 2nd and 3rd on the T-34. The declared weight of 31·5 long tons is difficult to reconcile with the increase in armour thickness and a slight lengthening of the hull, despite the reduction in height, although all information regarding this tank must be treated with reserve as very few were seen in service and there is no evidence that they replaced the T-34/85 to any marked extent. Indeed, it was rumoured that there had been considerable problems with the running gear and transmission and it is possible that T-44 was a test bed for a number of new ideas which were to be incorporated in a major redesign which was soon to follow.

T-54

The T-54 was introduced between 1946 and 1949 and it was soon evident that this was to be the replacement for T-34/85. A completely new design of turret mounting a 100-mm. gun was its most noticeable feature but in most other respects the influence of T-34 and T-44 are very much in evidence, and at 35 long tons, 7 ft. 10 ins. high and 29 ft. 7 ins. long overall, it is surprisingly small to anyone accustomed to tanks of similar capabilities elsewhere.

The hull is constructed from welded rolled plate and the sides are vertical except for a small overhang amidships to accommodate the turret ring. The interlocking joint between the glacis and nose plates to strengthen this vulnerable area is a clue to the improvement in engineering over previous designs. The driver's hatch is again on the left front of the hull roof and

there is an escape hatch in the floor between him and the gunner's position. A splash guard stretches the width of the glacis plate. The rear of the hull roof contains access plates for the power compartment and grilles for cooling air. Fuel and oil tanks, as well as stowage bins, are secured to the trackguards on either side and two brackets on the rear of the hull can be used either for smoke emitter cylinders, extra fuel drums, or both together.

The mechanic/driver's compartment contains the normal basic controls, although the steering levers have additional functions that will be described later. But there is a marked absence of other controls and gauges compared with modern tanks elsewhere, although unusual features include warning lights which

An early T-54 of the Egyptian Army destroyed during the Arab-Israeli war in 1967. (Photo: Interavia)

T-54A showing the mounting lugs welded on the nose plate for the attachment of a dozer blade, as well as the splash board on the glacis which was first introduced on the T-44. Note fume extractor fitted near the gun muzzle.

illuminate when the gun is traversed outside the width of the hull and remind the driver to make the appropriate allowances, and a gyroscopic drift indicator for navigation at night and under water. Another unusual feature which was first seen on T-44 is the 7·62-mm. MG (now an SGMT) on the right wall of the compartment and fired by a button on the top of the right hand steering lever. The seat is adjustable to allow the driver to sit "head-out", or fully down where he uses two periscopes. The space to his right is occupied by a fuel tank, the batteries, and ammunition for the 100-mm. gun.

The shape of the hemispherical turret has been aptly described as being like an egg, slightly flattened, and halved through its long axis. As such it represents a near ideal solution to the problem of providing the maximum protection for the minimum weight of armour but its internal volume is probably difficult to fill comfortably and economically with men and equipment. It is made from a single casting with a roof plate welded on, into which are fitted the two hatch assemblies. Some of the first vehicles seen had a slightly different, oval shape of turret with a small cutaway portion at the bottom rear, but these may have represented a pre-production series. A ventilator dome is on the top right and hand rails are welded on both sides of the turret for use by infantry. The commander and gunner are on the left of the gun, one behind the other, with the loader on the right. The main armament is a 100-mm. D-10T gun 1944 model, about 56 calibres long, and probably very similar to the D-10S mounted in the SU-100. In the case of the T-54A the gun barrel carries a fume extractor just behind the muzzle although the basic model of T-54 has a barrel of plain section except for a strengthening collar at the muzzle. The gun is mounted with the trunnions relatively far behind the turret front wall and it has an internal splash shield in place of a conventional mantlet. An elevation arc from $+17°$ to $-4°$ is available, the latter being too small by western standards. The breech ring contains a horizontally-sliding block and will be normally operated semi-automatically in that the block is opened and the case ejected onto the floor during run-out. The ammunition is fixed in design and probably includes a type of Armour Piercing Capped and HE for the earlier versions of gun. A rate of fire of 7 rounds per minute has been quoted but this seems very optimistic in the cramped space available to the loader. The second 7·62-mm. SGMT is mounted coaxially on the right of the 100-mm. cradle.

The main sight for the gunner is the TSh-22 articulated telescope and is similar in general design to that used in T-34/85. The range scales are on a ballistic

Smoke canisters are carried on brackets at the rear of this T-54A.

The interior of the driving compartment of a T-54A. The steering levers and foot controls are placed conventionally with the gear-change lever on the right. The two periscopes are below and forward of the hatch cover.

Czech T-54 tanks moving forward to a river crossing site with the folding schnorkel tube erected over the loader's periscope housing and with waterproofing equipment installed. The loader's cupola and the rear brackets for fuel drums appear to be different to those on T-54 tanks in Soviet service.
(Photo: Soldat und Technik)

Another rear view of a T-54A showing the schnorkel tube stowed beneath the smoke canisters.

Polish T-54A tanks taking part in an exercise involving a seaborne assault. *(Photo: Soldat und Technik)*

Polish T-54A tanks showing the excellent ballistic shape of the turret without the cut-away portion of the earliest version. The 12·7-mm. DShK anti-aircraft MG is mounted prominently in front of the loader's hatch. Note also the lightly armoured fuel tanks on the rear of the track guard and the hand-rails on the turret for use by mounted infantry.

graticule in the field of view and the magnification can be set at either 3·5 or 7 times. The front of the sight is protected by a long perspex cover. Semi-indirect or fully indirect fire is possible using a clinometer and an azimuth scale on the traverse ring. The gunner also has an episcope for general observation. Traverse and elevation of the turret is obtained by either manual or electrical control, with an over-riding facility for the commander, and it seems likely that the T-54A has an electro-hydraulic stabiliser in the elevation plane only which will permit fairly accurate firing on the move, providing that the driver maintains a sensibly constant speed without making sudden changes in direction. It seems likely that the principle of operation involves the measurement of vertical movements of the gun relative to a given datum by means of a rate gyro whose signals are amplified and then initiate the appropriate correcting signals to the elevating motor. When the firing switch is pressed the gearbox is automatically locked for the instant of firing and then drives the gun back to the angle it was laid at previously. A traverse lock is provided to secure the turret at the 6 or 12 o'clock positions for travelling out of action.

The commander has a rotatable cupola which is again very similar in design to that used on the later versions of T-34/85. The target designating sight TPK-1 is a bi-ocular instrument and incorporates a graticule which can be used as a crude stadiametric rangefinder and for correcting fire at long range. By rotating the cupola until the TPK-1 is aligned with a target and then pressing a line-up switch on the instrument and holding this firmly, the turret will traverse until it is on the line of sight defined by the commander. The commander gives a verbal description of the target which has then appeared in the field of view of the sighting telescope, the gunner makes a final lay against the appropriate range scale and fires. Two other episcopes flank the TPK-1 in the commander's cupola and a further two (unlike the T-34/85) are

provided in the hatch cover which hinges forward to open. He also operates the VHF radio equipment, assisted by the gunner. An inter-communication system is used within the tank and for the commander of infantry being carried on the outside of the vehicle, the earphones and laryngophone-type microphones being incorporated in the crash helmet worn by each crewman. The mounting for the rod antenna is left and forward of the commander's cupola.

The loader also has a rotating hatch assembly which incorporates a mounting and collimating sight for a 12·7-mm. DShK MG for use against low-flying aircraft. As such, this is an unusual arrangement in western eyes, where an AAMG is controlled by the commander, and implies that there is no question of the main armament having to be loaded at the same time. The gun is belt fed and the loader has presumably to expose much of his body in order to fire it. There is an observation periscope in front and slightly to the right of this hatch. Other features in the fighting compartment include a forced-draught ventilation system to clear gun fumes, as well as the usual stowage positions for ammunition and personal weapons. The main fuel tanks are immediately to the rear of the fighting compartment bulkhead, in the power and transmission compartment. About 180 imperial gallons of fuel are carried in all, using the internal tanks and tanks on the trackguards, although a further 88 gallon drum can be stowed on the rear of the hull, as already mentioned. Fully stowed thus, a T-54 has a remarkable range of about 380 miles on roads without refuelling.

The engine, again, is almost identical to that used in T-34 although the increase in width of the vehicle has enabled it to be mounted transversely, thus making a very economical use of the total volume available. Now designated V-54G, the four-stroke 12-cylinder 60° Vee diesel engine, with a capacity of 38·88 litres, develops 520 b.h.p. at 2,000 r.p.m. Starting is usually

A T-54A. Note the prominent gap between the first and second road wheels. The exhaust cowl is visible as the narrow oblong shape on the track guard just to the rear of the long stowage bin.

by an electric motor, although a compressed air system is available for emergencies or in very cold conditions. Air filtration is done in two stages, the first consisting of a centrifugal cleaner, which is kept clean by back pressure from the exhaust system, and the second of oil wetted elements. Lubrication is of the conventional dry sump type and includes a heater coil for use in cold weather, a similar heating element being also found in the pressurised cooling system. Both the oil cooler and coolant radiator are mounted horizontally above the gearbox. Exhaust gases are vented direct to atmosphere through a large cowl on the left trackguard.

Torque from the engine crankshaft is transmitted initially through a reduction unit which serves the double purpose of turning the drive through 180° and reducing its speed by 0·7:1. The clutch is of the multi-plate, steel on steel type and is attached to the gearbox casing: drive for the cooling fan is also tapped off at this point through a further friction clutch to avoid damaging the fan mechanism during sudden changes in engine speed. The main gearbox is manually operated and constant mesh in design providing five forward and one reverse gear with synchromesh on the top three forward ratios. Two steering boxes are fitted, one on either side of the gearbox, and are of the double stage planetary type with a single epicyclic geartrain and an interlocking clutch between the sun pinion and planet carrier. This arrangement enables the system to be used, not only for steering, but also as an auxiliary gearbox and main braking unit. The driver's steering brakes have three positions: when fully forward the interlocking clutches are engaged, the sun pinions and planet carriers rotate as one, the steering and main brakes are disengaged and drive is direct from the gearbox to the final reduction gears. If one lever is pulled back to the first position the appropriate clutch is disengaged and the tank turns in a constant radius. When both are applied in this manner a total reduction of 1·42:1 is obtained between the input and output shafts of the steering box which permits a brief increase in tractive effort without recourse to the main gearbox and is used to maintain momentum over minor obstacles and broken ground generally. If one lever is pulled fully back to the second position the main brake on that side is engaged but both clutch and steering brakes are disengaged and a skid turn is made in the appropriate direction, but if both are, or the foot brake is applied, the main brakes stop the vehicle, and if the steering levers are left in this position, act as parking brakes. Drive from the steering boxes to the sprockets is transmitted through a single stage reduction train with a ratio of 6·78:1.

The driving sprockets and tracks are of conventional design, the original Christie layout having been finally abandoned. However, the dry pins are still retained in the same simple and effective way as used on the T-34, in that the heads, which are on the inside of the track only, are driven back into position if they tend to work loose by being struck by a cammed surface on the final drive housings. The road wheels are double rimmed with rubber tyres and are suspended on transverse torsion bars with hydraulic shock absorbers on the first and fifth stations. While the T-54 has a number of innovations compared with T-34—gun and stabiliser, turret design, transmission and running gear—Soviet designers have had no

T-54A tanks at Check-point Charlie in Berlin in October 1961. A presentation of bouquets to the tank crews is in progress. The ventilation dome in front of the loader's cupola is a distinctive feature of the T-54 series. (Photo: Associated Press)

7

A Soviet T-54A used in the occupation of Prague in August 1968. The radio antenna is on the left of the commander's cupola. Two large fuel drums are carried in addition to the smoke canisters with the schnorkel tube secured across the top. (Photo: Keystone)

A T-55, successor to the T-54 series, on exercise prior to the invasion of Czechoslovakia in 1968. Note the absence of the loader's cupola with its AAMG. (Photo: dpa)

T-55 tanks wading a river during an exercise. The disturbance to the water surface caused by the engine exhaust gases can be seen to the left of the tubes of the two leading tanks.

A T-55 equipped both with a fuel drum and two smoke canisters moving up to embark on an assault raft.

compunction in retaining old and well-proven components and the sequence of development has clearly been continuous.

WATER CROSSING

Two major steps forward were now to be made, and although neither actually originated in the U.S.S.R., it was there that they were brought into wide-scale and routine use: underwater wading, and infra-red night fighting equipment.

The importance of moving armour across water obstacles in the van of an assault has been recognised for almost as long as tanks have been a practical proposition. The first tank floated across a reservoir near London in November 1918 and development continued in a number of countries, including the Soviet Union with its T-38 and T-40 light reconnaissance tanks. But if the tank is to be small in volume compared with the weight of the equipment inside—as most users demand—then it will not be inherently buoyant and requires additional equipment to make it so, such as the canvas screens used on the Sherman DD tanks. The crossing of water obstacles submerged therefore had a number of clear advantages and both Britain and Germany appear to have started work on the technique in the late thirties. A British A9 cruiser crossed under the River Stour in May 1940 but more urgent matters were at hand and the project was abandoned. Indeed the Germans were even then planning to launch some of their leading PzKpfw III and PzKpfw IV tanks for the assault on Britain from landing ships standing off-shore, using a crude schnorkel device consisting of a flexible tube attached to a pipe kept afloat by a buoy and to a maximum depth of 42 ft. When this assault landing (Operation Sealion) was abandoned the Germans used the technique once only when making a surprise crossing of the River Bug on the first day of Operation Bar-

barossa against Russia.* The matter appears to have rested there, although some limited trials were carried out with Tiger tanks, until the Russians crossed the Vistula and Bug in 1944—in the opposite direction—when it is said that the T-34s waded using flexible exhaust pipes attached to floating bags and T-44s used two rigid vertical tubes, one for aspiratory air for the engine and crew and the other for the exhausts. Once again the matter seems to have rested, this time until 1958 when an increasing number of T-54s were seen using this technique.

The problem of sealing a tank against the ingress of water is relatively simple, as good ballistic and gas protection demands the minimum of apertures anyway. But the hatches and mantlet require additional sealing and the turret ring may be sealed using an inflatable rubber ring such as has been used on Centurion. The gun muzzle also must be plugged but this can be simply removed by firing a blank round. The engine compartment can either be allowed to flood or sealed by rubber matting as is the case with Soviet tanks. Exhausts are fitted with flutter valves which are held open by gas pressure when the engine is running but are closed automatically by springs should the engine stall. Aspiratory air is drawn through a narrow tube which is fitted over the loader's periscope mounting from which the instrument has been removed and it is steadied by stay wires. A marker buoy is usually attached to the tank tow rope via a light line attached to the top of the tube to facilitate recovery if the tank fails to complete the crossing. The radio antenna is also transferred to the top of the tube so that the crew can receive external guidance en route. This preparatory work is done in hides a kilometre or so from the crossing point. Using

*June 22, 1941. The equipment was used by the leading tanks of 18th Panzer Division north of Brest-Litovsk and enabled them to move through 13 feet of water—Editor.

this method the T-54 can traverse wide rivers up to a depth of about 18 ft. after a preparation time of between 30 and 60 minutes, depending on the state of modification of the vehicle. But while there are relatively few problems in flopping a tank into the water, the actual crossing and getting out on the far bank is rather more difficult. Special preparation may be necessary on that bank to reduce the slope which will be awash with liquid mud as soon as the first vehicle has left and assistance may often be necessary at this juncture. With this in view, the T-54T recovery vehicle will usually cross first, equipped with winch and a specially wide schnorkel tube to enable the crew to climb in and out while submerged. A check of the bed of the waterway will also be necessary to establish that it is clear of obstacles and reasonably hard, because although submerged the vehicle acquires a certain buoyancy, thereby reducing ground pressure and therefore traction, while rolling resistance is increased by the tracks becoming tighter and through the displacement of the water. A further limitation is the speed of the current which will tend to push the tank down-stream. These checks will normally be done by specially trained and equipped engineers well in advance of the arrival of the tanks.

A large number of T-54 tanks were either modified for this task or had the necessary equipment installed *ab initio*. The schnorkel tubes could be carried in unit transport but this is normally at a premium and it is probably more usual to stow the tubes on the tanks

themselves, in two sections, either above or below the rear fuel tanks. Crews are given comprehensive training in escape drills culminating in an actual crossing in a tank equipped with a wide tower, similar to that used on the ARV.

FIGHTING AT NIGHT

As with under-water crossing, so also with night fighting equipment: the feasibility of near infra-red devices had been realised for a number of years* but the equipping of T-54 tanks, again in 1958, heralded its first large scale use on the battlefield. A typical installation consists of a searchlight with a filter that blocks out the visible component of the spectrum but allows the longer wavelengths through. The reflected infra-red radiation is restored into a visible image in a converter tube in the special sight. A range of about 1,000 metres seems usual with the searchlight proper but only about 30 or 40 metres for a converted headlamp, although this is sufficient to drive by. Used against an opponent who is not similarly equipped the effect of being able to manoeuvre and shoot in apparently complete darkness is devastating, but where both sides have it a deadly game of "chicken" ensues. As a passive sight can detect an active source of radiation, such as a searchlight, at a greater range than the latter is able to

*The German UHU equipment being an example in which the battlefield was illuminated by a 60-cm. IR searchlight and tanks operated using passive viewers.

Top left: *T-62 tanks discharging a dense screen of partially burnt fuel oil from their exhausts.*

Bottom left: *A Top Sergeant commander of a T-54 using his TPK-1 target designating sight.*   (Photo: Camera Press)

Below: *A T-54A(M) which mounts full IR night fighting equipment with the main searchlight mounted on a bracket on the turret and connected to the gun barrel by a parallelogram linkage. A smaller projector is mounted on the commander's cupola for shorter range surveillance. The long slit for the gunner's sighting telescope is also visible to the right of the 100-mm. gun. Note also the two driving lights, one white, one infra-red: the front crewman is sitting on the latter.*   (Photo: Camera Press)

Two T-55 tanks from the Kiev Military District lead a column of motorised infantry which includes two BTR-50p APCs. An additional small IR projector can be seen to the left and below the main searchlight.

A T-54A(M) in Prague 1968. The long equilibrator tubes needed to balance the 12·7 mm. AAMG are visible under the barrel.

(Photo: Keystone)

11

A sabotaged bridge in Czechoslovakia 1968 allows one to see the plan view of a T-54A(M). The shape of the two turret hatches can be clearly seen, together with the "lift and swing" hatch for the driver. (Photo: dpa)

illuminate, each side tries to avoid using active sources as long as possible in the hope that the other will give his position away first. In general terms, therefore, the advantage tends to lie with the defence.

A typical installation on the T-54 has a large searchlight mounted on the right hand forward part of the turret, connected to the gun for elevation by means of a parallelogram linkage, a smaller light and viewer on the front of the commander's cupola for short range surveillance, and two driving lights, one white and one infra-red, together with an adapted periscope for the driver himself. Again, it is possible that this installation was a retrospective modification on many tanks although all built since the early sixties appear to have had it included in the basic specification.

A Soviet T-54(X), recognizable by its flush loader's hatch and by the fact that the main IR searchlight is attached to the gun barrel itself. The T-54B is similar except it has the normal cupola for the loader. (Photo: Camera Press)

T-55 AND T-62

Among these various changes to the basic design it became evident that a new version altogether had appeared and was in production under the designation of T-55. The first sign was the disappearance of the loader's cupola and the AAMG on most models, together with the ventilation dome on the turret. Other changes could include further development of the power plant and gun—both basically old designs by now—stabilization of the gun in two planes, and the stowage of more ammunition, as well as a form of over-pressurization ventilation system to enable the tank to operate in an area contaminated by nuclear and chemical weapons. It seems likely also that the original smoke emitters have been replaced by a method of injecting vaporized fuel into the engine exhaust, and a T-55 using this system when moving at speed is reminiscent of a warship making smoke. Although it does little to conceal the laying tank it provides a reasonable screen behind which others can manoeuvre or infantry advance and has the advantage of being cheap.

In 1961 an unmistakably new version appeared called T-62. This tank probably mounts a 115-mm. gun with a smooth bore—which could indicate the use of fin-stabilized ammunition—and the fume extractor has been moved further back from the muzzle. The shape of the turret has been modified, the hull is a little longer and the overall height lowered. The suspension has been altered to accommodate this increase in length and there are now prominent gaps between the last three road wheels. But in most other respects it is very similar in appearance to its predecessors.

VARIANTS

The use of the T-54T armoured recovery vehicle in assisting at water crossing operations has already been noted, although it is also used for the more mundane field tasks. A less radical modification consists of the fitting of a dozer blade onto the nose plate of any standard gun tank. This T-54/BTU *(Buldosernoje Tankowoje Ustrojstwo)* is used for digging defensive positions and the preparation of river crossing sites as well as for clearing rubble and other obstacles. The height of the blade is controlled hydraulically and a shoe protrudes from the centre, probably to define the maximum depth of cut. Standard gun tanks can also be fitted with PT-54 mine rollers which are similar in concept to those used with the T-34. A heavy frame is attached to the front of the hull and two sets of four serrated wheels are aligned in front and in line with the tank tracks. Another version may consist of two serrated ploughs which can be lowered hydraulically in front of the tank tracks.

Most of the waterways in Central Europe consist of drainage ditches or steep-sided streams, rather than rivers or canals, and it would be either impossible or uneconomic to cross them under-water. These will therefore be crossed with the aid of the T-54/MTU *(Mostoukladtschik Tankowoje Ustrojstwo)* which consists of a turret-less T-54 onto which is mounted a rigid bridge span some 43 ft. long. On reaching the

A T-55 fording a shallow stream. As well as the absence of the loader's cupola and the ventilation dome, note the change in design of the commander's cupola and his new sight.

T-62 tanks marching past at the end of the Warsaw Pact exercises in 1967.   (Photo: Associated Press)

13

The basic resemblance to the T-34/85 is evident in the interim T-44 which mounted the well-proven 85-mm. gun.

(Photo: Lehmanns Verlag)

T-62 "953", with its gun traversed to the rear, being pelted by an angry crowd in Prague. Note the sloping and flush-fitting loader's hatch.

(Photo: dpa)

T-62 tanks in parade livery marching past Lenin's tomb in Moscow. The change to a circular aperture for the gunner's sighting telescope can be seen on the nearer vehicle.

A T-54/MTU on the move with its 43 ft. rigid bridge span. (Photo: Lehmanns Verlag)

obstacle the span is winched forward on a launching frame pivotting on the forward end of the hull roof until the nose of the bridge grounds on the far bank. The frame is then disengaged and the launcher either crosses the bridge or waits to recover it after other combat units have used it. An obvious advantage of this method of launching is that the operation has a better chance of remaining undetected, although, against this, the length of span that can be carried and launched in this way is obviously less than that for one of scissors construction, for example.

The ZSU-57-2 (*Zenitny Samokhodnaya Ustanovka*) is another radical conversion in which a shortened T-54 chassis with only four road wheels mounts a light, open-topped turret containing twin 57-mm. anti-aircraft guns. But the lack of a sophisticated fire control equipment, and the more recent appearance of the ZSU-23-4 based on the PT-76 chassis and having its own radar set, indicates that the ZSU-57-2 is probably obsolescent, although it still could be a potent weapon against APCs.

Trials may also have been carried out on an assault gun version based on the T-54 chassis but it seems likely that the standard tank is now considered to be more effective.

TACTICAL DOCTRINE

The strategic background to Russian tank design has already been outlined and one is left in no doubt that armoured forces would play a leading part in any future war, which could well involve the use of chemical and nuclear weapons at a very early stage. Their excellent mobility which is enhanced by a relative independence of bridging and night fighting equipment—coupled with good protection and fire-power—make the Soviet medium tanks ideal weapons for this type of war in view of Frunze's exhortations to operate offensively as soon as possible. Armoured forces are trained to exploit the shock and surprise of an enemy subjected to massive nuclear and chemical strikes by manoeuvring boldly, ignoring open flanks and gaps between formations and bypassing minor opposition in the best *blitzkrieg* tradition. Only when organized defences cannot be bypassed will attacks be mounted deliberately but, again, these will be planned and executed with the least possible delay, the troops often being deployed

directly off the line of march. A standard of 100 kilometres (62 miles) in 24 hours has often been stated to be the necessary speed against opposition but this seems unduly optimistic by any criteria, even in the light of the Manchurian campaign already quoted. Momentum will be maintained by the use of parachute and helicopter-borne troops to seize key objectives ahead of the advance and cause confusion among the defenders while the main forces will be deployed in echelon, so that when the leading elements suffer heavy casualties or run out of fuel and ammunition fresh formations can be passed through to take over the lead.

Reconnaissance troops also operate well ahead of the main body to find the enemy, bypass him if possible or pin him until an attack can be mounted. These forces will be equipped typically with the amphibious BTR-4OP (or PB) scout cars, whose four main wheels can be supplemented by a further four lowered hydraulically to assist in crossing soft or rough ground, and the PT-76 light amphibious tank, simple and lightly armoured, mounting a low-velocity 76-mm. in a conical turret. Although the mobility of the latter is excellent, particularly in the water where it uses a very effective hydro-jet propulsion system, its effectiveness as a reconnaissance vehicle must be qualified by the apparent lack of any night fighting equipment and the fact that the commander also acts as gunner. Specialist engineer and chemical-cum-radiological survey teams are often attached to these forces which may also be supported by medium tanks.

Once the enemy is found, tanks will rarely stop to fire—hence the use of stabilizing equipment—as a large volume of somewhat inaccurate fire from a mass of moving tanks is considered to be more effective, both physically and psychologically, than better aimed shots from static positions at longer ranges; indeed, even pinpoint targets will rarely be engaged at more than 1,000 metres range and crews are probably still reminded that the tank track is itself a very important weapon when closing with the enemy. If tanks in the second echelon are available within range, however, they may be used to fire HE indirect in support of the attack. Tactical manoeuvres are usually carried out according to strict and well-practised drills and radio commands will then be limited to pre-arranged codewords. Tanks will

15

A T-54/MTU crossing the bridge that it has just laid. The launching frame is clearly visible.

normally lead the assault with the infantry in their APCs following closely behind. If the opposition is light the infantrymen will remain in their vehicles to fire their automatic weapons through ports in the side armour but will dismount for an assault if more determined resistance has to be overcome.

The defensive battle is regarded only as an unavoidable pause before the resumption of the offensive. Wherever possible the tanks are dug into ambush positions, preferably on reverse slopes or to the flanks with planned secondary positions available, although a large proportion will be held in depth to act as a counter-attack force.

In theory these tactics seem unbeatable but their effectiveness is almost certainly diminished by an over-centralized command structure and a rigidity in putting them into practice which would lead to opportunities being missed and costly or ineffective actions pursued. The constant pressure to advance regardless gives commanders at the lower levels little chance to reconnoitre and plan, while the need to conserve the resources of the formations following behind will probably lead to their moving in vulnerable columns rather than being dispersed. All these factors favour a defender who is prepared to stand firm.

The actual use of the modern Soviet mediums so far has fortunately fallen well short of these aggressive tactics. Both T-44s and T-54s were used to suppress the uprising in Hungary in 1956, suffering a number of casualties at the hands of the insurgents in the bitter street fighting, and T-54s were again in evidence

The T-62 mounting a new 115-mm. gun.

in Berlin in the autumn of 1961, including an anxious few hours when they confronted American M48A1 tanks of 40th Armor at Checkpoint Charlie. The Six Day war in 1967 saw T-54s and T-55s pitted against military forces for the first time but their performance against Centurions armed with the 105-mm. gun, M48s and even modified Shermans was indifferent enough to give Soviet designers and users some cause for concern; and indignation when the tanks captured intact have been used by Israeli crews. All three types were represented during the invasion and occupation of Czechoslovakia in 1968.

It is notoriously difficult to obtain reliable data on Russian equipment but tens of thousands of these tanks must have been built for the Soviet Army alone, apart from those supplied to other countries. As well as all the Warsaw Pact armies, customers have included Cuba, North Korea, Finland, Yugoslavia, Iraq, Syria, the United Arab Republic, India, Algeria and Morocco.* China has built a number of T-54As under the designation of T-59 and sold some to Pakistan. Otherwise, as only Czechoslovakia, Poland and possibly East Germany have limited armament industries in Eastern Europe, the Soviet Union is in the happy position of being able to maintain long production runs with consequently low unit costs and having a number of clients who often have little choice but to accept obsolescent or surplus equipment.

*The Military Balance 1969-70, Institute for Strategic Studies, London.

The T-54/T armoured recovery vehicle with its wide-diameter schnorkel tube in the travelling position.
(Photo: Soldat und Technik)

Standardization to this extent also eases the logistic load within the Warsaw Pact itself, a situation which its western counterpart may envy with reason.

The modern Soviet mediums appear to combine the attributes of mobility, firepower and protection in a remarkable if rather austere form. Reliability is inherent in the design of components which are both well-tried and under-stressed. The wide radius of action and the ability to cross water obstacles and fight at night favour the aggressive and wide-ranging tactics in nuclear and chemical conditions which feature regularly in the settings for Warsaw Pact

The PT-54 mine roller equipment based on an obsolescent T-54.   (Photo: Lehmanns Verlag)

ZSU-57-2 self-propelled AA guns based on a shortened T-54 chassis with four instead of five road wheel positions.

(Photo: Associated Press)

exercises, and there is no reason to think that the parameters for the successor to these vehicles will be essentially different or that revolution rather than steady evolution will mark its design. Arguments that a tank must be capable of engaging enemy armour at long ranges, thereby requiring sophisticated fire control devices, a large load of ammunition, a high rate of fire and the ability to take up hull down positions by virtue of having a large angle of depression for the main armament, are all probably irrelevant in Soviet eyes. More pertinent criticisms can be levelled, however, at the extremly cramped conditions in the fighting compartments which must inevitably lead to losses in efficiency in protracted operations, as well as the vulnerability of ammunition and fuel, bearing in mind that much of the latter is not stowed under armour.

Continuous development and the ruthless rejection of inessentials have been the hallmarks of an almost unbroken series of successful designs which originated in the workshop of an American engineer in the early thirties, led the world in the forties, and have been the spearhead of one of the most potent forces in the world ever since.

A Chinese version of the T-54A sold to Pakistan under the designation of T-59. The Chinese may also have developed a considerably smaller version of this tank although visually it retains nearly all the characteristics of the original.

(Photo: Associated Press)

TECHNICAL DATA ON T-54A

Dimensions and Weights

Length overall	: 29 ft. 7 in.
Length of hull overall	: 20 ft. 7 in.
Width overall	: 10 ft. 9 in.
Height to top of commander's cupola	: 7 ft. 10 in.
Distance between track centres	: 8 ft. 8 in.
Ground clearance	: 1 ft. 5 in.
Track width	: 1 ft. 10 in.
Length of track on ground	: 12 ft. 7 in.
Inside diameter of turret ring	: 5 ft. 11 in.
Weight combat loaded	: between 34·9 and 35·4 long tons
Ground pressure	: 11·4 lbs./sq. in.

Fuel and Ammunition Stowage

Fuel (Imperial Galls)
Internal tanks	:	117
External tanks	:	66
Rear drum(s)	:	88
Total		271 imperial gallons

Ammunition (rounds)

100 mm.	: 34 (20 HE, 14 AP)
12·7 mm.	: 500
7·62 mm. SGMT	: 3000
7·62 mm. for personal weapons	: 300
Grenades	: 20

Performance (all figures approximate)

Fuel consumption:
Roads	: 0·7 m.p.g.
Cross country	: 1·0 m.p.g.

Range using all available fuel:
Roads	: 385 miles
Cross country	: 270 miles

Speeds:
Maximum	: 30 m.p.h.
Roads	: 21 m.p.h.
Cross country	: 16 m.p.h.

Maximum slope	: 30° (58%)
Maximum ditch width	: 9 ft.
Vertical Step	: 2 ft. 7 in.

T 48 Prototype with original cupola and A/A machine-gun and with original 90-mm. gun, showing details of suspension.

Photo:—Courtesy Chrysler Corporation

The M48-M60 Series of Main Battle Tanks

IN BATTLE

THE M48 originally was intended for use by United States forces in the Korean War had that war continued for longer than it did. However, the M48 did not become available until the war was over. M48 tanks, nevertheless, have since seen combat in traditional tank rôles in the hands of soldiers of other lands which received them from the United States by purchase or under military assistance programs. Among these were the Pakistanis, who used them in the short war against India in 1965.

After an advance into Pakistan north of Ferozepore on September 6 of that year, the Indians were driven back by Pakistani pressure. The Indians retreated to their starting point at Khem Karan but set a trap. In the area of Assal Uttar there was a river on the Indian left flank and a canal on their right. The Indians cut the canal in order to flood its immediate vicinity which made possible the channeling of the Pakistani advance. The story, somewhat extravagantly told by D. R. Mankekar in *Twenty Two Fateful Days* (Manaktaton, Bombay, 1966) continues:

"On September 8 morning, the enemy came with two squadrons of Chaffes (*sic*) and one of Pattons on a rekke-in-force (15 tanks) when he hit against our infantry positions on the main road. The rekke-in-force went back after a clash.

"That night the enemy returned with a whole combat group (one Patton regiment and two squadrons of Chaffes). It was a critical night, as he had brought armour in force and the defenders could not use tanks . . . With their infra-red eyes, the Pattons could see, but not our Shermans, which were 'blind' at night. But the Indian artillery stepped into the breach and did a grand job.

"On September 9, an Indian armoured brigade was rushed to the scene and straightaway . . . disposed . . . The entire battle plan formed into a horseshoe, into which the enemy was to be enticed.

"That day the Pakistanis launched yet another—the third—attack on our infantry position, which too was flung back. On September 10, the enemy came up in full force, with his infantry rolling up immediately behind a phalanx of armour.

"The main battle was joined at 08.30. Having failed to pierce our infantry position, the enemy armour tried a flanking movement, a sort of right hook, with a view to getting behind the infantry position. There, lying in wait, further behind, almost concealed in tall standing sugar cane crop, was a squadron of Centurions. The moment the line of Pattons turned and exposed their broadside, the Centurions opened up and threw the enemy into confusion. Here it was that we captured 15 Pak tanks intact, with their engines running and crews jumping out to surrender.

19

The production T48 with gun secured in the travel lock and turret to the rear, showing blackout lights and telephone box.
Photo—U.S. Ordnance Corps

"The enemy made a second, this time a wider flanking movement to get at our gun positions which had played havoc with them, and then ran into the jaws of another line of our Centurions . . . Having to fight in sugar cane and maize fields and peer through a 9 ft. high, thick, ripening standing crop, the Patton's visibility was reduced to a thousand yards, which is a Centurion's range, and thus it lost its extra advantages. Then again, quite a few of the heavy Pattons got bogged down into the submerged soft soil following the letting out of the water from the Rohi (canal) by our forces.

"This epic battle . . . comprised a series of six engagements, with which the Pakistanis were seeking a breakthrough. On the last day was fought the clincher and the fiercest of the series, when Pakistan's 4th Cavalry (50 tanks) was trapped and completely annihilated and the rest of the armoured division badly mauled.

"In the entire series, the Pakistanis lost 97 tanks counted as destroyed, disabled and captured . . ."

Contrast this poor showing by the Pakistani M48 tanks with the brilliant demonstration by Israeli armoured troops in the Six Day War in 1967. At the western end of the Gaza Strip in early June was a formidable Egyptian position. The Egyptian 7th Division had its three brigades in line parallel to the main highway south of Rahfa straight west to El Arish. Two additional battalions were east of Rahfa. A full brigade of artillery was located behind the infantry. West of there was the Jerardi hedgehog within which there were 30 bunkered Shermans, a full division plus two brigades and a hundred Stalin 3

Top view of the T48 with all hatches open and driver's periscopes lowered.
Photo—U.S. Ordnance Corps

(JS3) tanks in line behind the infantry trenches. There were deep minefields in front of the trenches and anti-tank batteries in pits extended along the entire front.

Instead of driving head on, the Israelis planned to send a brigade of armour and two battalions of paratroops serving as armoured infantry to probe through the dunes for an open flank to the south. The armoured brigade had a Patton battalion on the right and a Centurion battalion on the left. Colonel Uri Baron was the brigade commander and he took personal command of the Pattons. What took place then is described in *Swift Sword* by Brigadier General S. L. A. Marshall (American Heritage Publishing Company, New York, 1967):

"While Baron and his tanks looked on, waves of Israeli-built Fougas, flying very low, came on for a thirty-minute strike with rockets against the artillery bases . . . The Egyptians put up a storm of flak, but it was a perfect strafe, and not one Fouga got hit. The air force, destroying two-thirds of the fieldpieces based near Rahfa, made two hundred sorties on June 5 . . .

"Baron's Pattons then ran forward, seeking the soft spot south of the mined front. The Fougas roared back to pound the guns again as the tanks came even with the defended line, so that there would be no interval between the shock dealt to the artillery and the attempt to breach the infantry position. The company commander stood up in the turret of the leading Patton. The tank hit a mine and exploded into flames, killing both captain and crew. Their deaths saved the others. The tanks that followed saw at once that the captain had made too short a turn. Guiding on the pyre, they swung farther south through the dunes before veering west, then north, on a hook around the entrenchments.

"Trailing after the tanks, using the same lanes, came the armoured infantry in half-tracks. Already the movement started to fall apart. The armour was charging on to strike deep and finish off the artillery position. The infantry was to double back and assault the main trench line from the rear. Traversing the loose dunes, however, the half-tracks simply could not keep the pace. Engineers had the mission of clearing a lane through the minefields.

"Completing the destruction of the artillery, the armour engaged a battalion of Stalins, destroyed most of them with gunfire at short range. A bit giddy with their success, both battalions ran on to attack infantry and machine-gun emplacements farther west. That was a mistake and not according to their instructions; one battalion was supposed to turn and help the armoured infantry in its mop-up of the entrenched line . . .

"After neutralizing some of the positions in the Egyptian brigade farthest south, the paratroops of one battalion had moved on north to attack the central perimeter. At that point their luck ran out. They became isolated and immobilized by fire on the ground where the two brigades joined.

". . . The battalion of armour that had careened on was directed to reverse and carry out the mission as planned.

"Colonel Baron's tanks had already blasted the six battalions of 122-mm. and 100-mm. artillery pieces, as well as the 85-mm. and 57-mm. anti-tank batteries, to complete the destruction the Fougas has begun. Baron

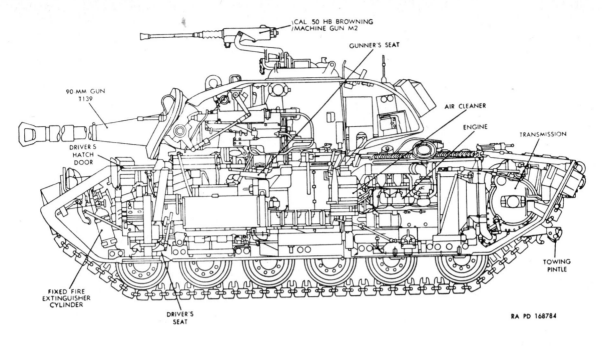

Cross section of the M48 with original cupola and A/A gun.   Drawing—U.S. Ordnance Corps

The T31 computer used in the M48 tank makes the corrections required for various types of ammunition.   Photo—U.S. Army

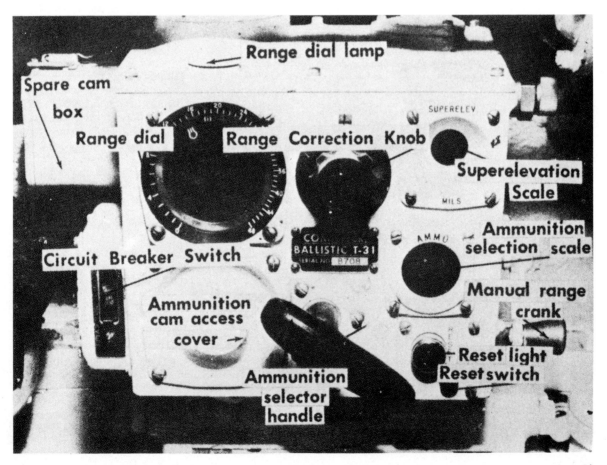

Rear view of the T48 with turret transversed to the right. In this view the engine compartment louvers and exhausts are clearly visible.
Photo—U.S. Ordnance Corps

now heard the distress calls and the new order on his command radio. His Pattons were close to the scene. . . . With his battalion well collected and in the right place, Baron decided he must move to the rescue, though uninvited. From the rear his tanks destroyed the greater part of a brigade of eighteen hundred men. The fight to save the isolated battalion lasted ninety minutes, ending around 17·00 . . ."

In Viet Nam, the use by U.S. forces of M48 and M60 tanks has been limited to less traditional tank rôles, partly because of terrain, partly because of the guerrilla character of the war and partly because of bridge limitations. In that country, the Delta region is flat but cut up by rivers and a dense network of canals. North of Saigon, the ground gradually rises within 50 miles toward the highlands and there are extensive forests and rubber plantations. The southern portion of the central plateau in the highland area near the

Laotian and Cambodian borders is good tank country but the coastal plain is cut at intervals by mountain ridges. It and the northern two-thirds of the country which comprises jungle-covered mountains are poor tank country.

Lack of manoeuvre space thus limited the use of medium or main battle tanks. The M113 Armoured Personnel Carriers because of their amphibian character were used as light tanks while the medium tanks acted as a base of fire for them. Later, when tree-levelling devices such as Rome Plows were introduced, a few tactical changes took place. The Rome Plow originally was a standard commercial tractor modified at a plant in Rome, Georgia, to enable it to cut down the jungle growth that covers so much of Viet Nam. This reduced the number of possible enemy hiding places and also provided cleared areas on the sides of roads. The plows also were used by engineer troops to lead the way into the jungle, crushing bunkers and tunnels. They were followed by infantry in armoured personnel carriers and by armoured engineer vehicles or medium tanks. Because of the short life of the Rome Plow under such conditions of use, a simpler method was devised. A 225-ft long three-ton Navy anchor chain was hooked to the rear ends of two M48A3 tanks and stretched tight just off the ground to level foliage and brush. When so used, the M113 Armoured Personnel Carriers provided flank and rear security while a third M48A3 acted as point.

M48 or Patton series tanks are to be found in the armies of Greece, Israel, Italy, Jordan, Norway, Pakistan and Spain. The Israelis have upgunned their M48A2s with the British 105-mm. guns with which the Super Shermans are armed and have substituted diesel engines.

M48 DEVELOPMENT

The T48, as it was known originally, was initiated in December 1950 by letter contract awarded to the Chrysler Corporation. In March 1951, the Fisher Body Division of General Motors Corporation and the Ford Motor Company were awarded letter contracts for supplemental production and in October 1954 Chrysler received another contract for additional vehicles. Deliveries began in April 1952 and were completed in May 1956. These were the M48C (training type), M48 and M48A1. Standardization as the M48 had taken place in May 1953 despite the fact that tests had disclosed many defects.

The Controller General of the United States and his General Accounting Office are the watchdogs for Congress over governmental expenditures. In a report to Congress in 1960 the Controller General pointed out that there were serious defects impairing the operation and maintenance of the M48 and M48A1 Full Tracked Medium Gun Combat Tanks, to use their full name. These defects were found in initial models and throughout production and continued to exist in spite of numerous and costly modifications over the period 1951-58. In fact, it was held that "Initial production vehicles were defective to such an extent that they were not acceptable even for training purposes." The Controller General also reported that the situation was due to the practice of "contracting for volume production prior to adequate assurances

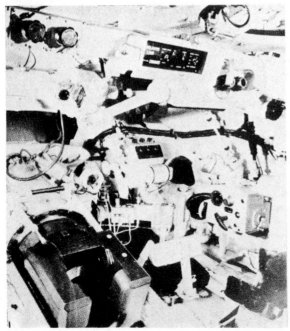

Gunner's position in M48 medium tank on lower right the ammunition selector lever is apparent on the T31 Computer.   Photo:—U.S. Army

that identified defects could be corrected during production or by subsequent modifications."

Tracks were thrown, the rangefinders could not be used by everyone even with normal vision and originally the tanks could be shifted into reverse while the vehicle was in motion. This last was a cause for much mechanical breakdown and later production was modified to prevent it. Despite limited usage the tanks frequently were out of commission due to breakdowns in engines, transmission, tracks and suspension, with an average of 2·7 failures for every 100 miles of operation. The Army insisted that the problems were due mainly to improper maintenance, failure to follow instruction manuals and poor driving habits, all of which probably were true.

The Army accepted responsibility based on the premise that the Korean War had justified crash procurement although most of the vehicles were delivered after hostilities in Korea had ceased in mid-1953.

This report by the Controller General, although critical, must be viewed in the proper perspective. It is perhaps the first specific analysis of defects in a given series of tanks to be made public anywhere in the world, although the report on *Wartime Tank Production* presented to Parliament in England in July 1946 had been even more critical but on a broader base. Most tracklaying vehicles must be properly cared for and maintained or they will exhibit similar defects, a well-established fact not yet learned by commanders who lack tank experience or who are unable to enforce discipline.

The principal problem of a design nature which was encountered was in the track compensating idler spindle. Changes in this and in the engine and transmission were made with the resulting vehicle produced as the M48A2. Alco Products Inc. received a contract for these in November 1955 and additional contracts were awarded Chrysler beginning in May 1957. A new problem arose in the M48A2 in the engine fan rotor which had a tendency to disintegrate, but this too finally was corrected.

The M48 had a low operating radius. Jettison fuel tanks were added but only to 1800 vehicles. These were among those furnished to Jordan. Reports from the Six Day War indicated that these supplementary fuel tanks presented a tremendous fire hazard in combat to vehicles so equipped. Fuel capacity was increased in the M48A2. Failures in the tank commander's override control also were corrected in the M48A2.

The tank commander's machine-gun was intended for use against both ground and aerial targets. This had been one of the significant reasons given for the development of the M48 over the M47. The original cupolas designed for the M48 would not fit and changes had to be made in the turret casting. Thus the early vehicles did not have the commander's cupola which has become standard on all U.S. vehicles. This commander's cupola ·50 calibre machine-gun was to have had an elevation range of —11° to +60°, but as produced the upper limit was only 50° and therefore the gun could not be used for anti-aircraft fire. In addition the cupola had dead spots in rotation.

Modifications to correct all shortcomings were made by Chrysler, U.S. Industries, Inc. and Lima

The M48 driver's instruments and hatch cover lever were located on his right. This view also shows the right periscope holder.
Photo—Courtesy Chrysler Corporation

Expendable roller mine clearing device developed for use with standard M48 tanks. Photo—U.S. Corps of Engineers

One of the Pakastani M48 tanks out of action at Assal Uttar in 1965.
Photo—Courtesy Tyler Segar.

In spite of the increase in height the new commander's cupola on the M48A1 was a distinct improvement. Photo—U.S. Ordnance Corps

Tank Depot, the two latter again doing work which already supposedly had been done.

The final cost per vehicle is very difficult to determine. The initial cost is estimated at $210,000 but to this must be added the cost of some $13,000 per vehicle up to 1956, and from total subsequent contract costs it is estimated that the total additional cost would be about $20,000, making the final cost per vehicle close to a quarter of a million dollars. To this must be added the cost of spare parts made obsolete by the production of an entirely new part to make a given correction.

M48 DESCRIPTION

The M48 has an ellipsoid cast hull with a plate bottom and an ellipsoid cast turret. It is supported on a torsion bar suspension with six forged aluminium bogie wheels and five support rollers per side. The hull is divided into three compartments, the driving compartment in front for the driver, the engine compartment in the rear and the fighting compartment in the turret in the centre for the commander, gunner and loader. A rotatable commander's cupola with machine-gun is mounted on the right side of the turret roof in the early production vehicles and a large commander's cupola is provided in the later models. The driver controls the vehicle with a rectangular steering-wheel which resembles the pilot's control on a jet airliner. There is no bow machine-gun.

The commander stands on the tank commander's platform or is seated. The gunner's seat is to the right of the 90-mm. gun in front of the tank commander, while the loader is seated on the left of the gun or stands.

The 90-mm. M41 gun comprises the tube, bore evacuator, blast deflector and breech mechanism in Combination Mount M87 in the M48, M48A1 and

Side view of the M48A1 with the small tension adjusting idler clearly visible near the drive sprocket. Photo—U.S. Ordnance Corps

M48C. In later models, the mount has variations of several types. All consist of a gun shield and cradle with a coaxial ·30 calibre machine-gun on the left side of the 90-mm. gun. The gun mount supports the gun in trunnion bearings and provides attachments for the breech operating and firing mechanisms for both guns and the recoil guards. The bore evacuator is a thin walled cylinder fitted around the forward end of the gun tube. Eight holes are drilled in the bore and slanted at an angle of 30° toward the muzzle. After firing, the resultant vacuum draws the air out of the tube so that the fumes, which are toxic, do not escape into the turret when the breech opens automatically to eject the case after firing. This breech block is a vertical sliding wedge type. The gun tube is quickly replaceable.

Percussion firing by electric solenoid is used. Three inches from the end of counter recoil after 12 inches of recoil the return is buffered so that the gun goes back into battery without shock. There is a replenisher assembly which takes care of the expansion of the concentric hydrospring recoil cylinder oil through heating from firing.

The bore is 14ft 9 ins long (or 48 calibres). Elevation —9° to +20°. The various forms of ammunition and their muzzle velocities are:

HE and WP 2400 f/s (high explosive and white phosphorus smoke)
AP   3050 f/s (armour piercing)
HVAP   4050 f/s (high velocity armour piercing)
HVAP-PS   4100 f/s (high velocity armour piercing super shot)
HEAT   2800 f/s (high explosive antitank)

Practice and blank rounds also are available. A canister round was developed for use in Viet Nam in 1968 and in 1969 a fixed round (flamethrower) made a flamethrower out of every tank gun. Instead of the customary "rod" of flamethrower fuel, the new round bursts into flame on arriving at target.

There are storage spaces for 19 rounds on the left of the driver and 11 rounds on the right with six rounds in the turret floor beneath the gun. There is space for 16 rounds vertically along the turret ring and there is an eight round ready rack in the turret. The 90-mm. round is long, and handling it in the turret of a moving tank is an operation requiring care, tending to slow the rate of fire.

M48A1 medium tank fitted with a commercial 2000 watt searchlight.
Photo—Armor Magazine

A stereo rangefinder graduated from 500 to 4,800 yards is operated by the tank commander. It transmits range data mechanically to a ballistic computer. This range datum is modified by ammunition and ballistic corrections which are manually applied by the gunner to the computer at his right. This results in what is called the super-elevation angle (the angle between the line of bore and the line of sight—in other words, the amount of parallax). This angle is transmitted electrically (or mechanically) through the ballistic drive (a mechanical linkage) to the periscope sight and the rangefinder. The computer has an ammunition selector handle providing for six changes of ammunition by means of different shaped cams. Range corrections can be made for air density, temperatures (ambient, powder and tube), tube wear, variations in lots of ammunitions, etc.

The gunner has one control handle in front of him; a grip with a trigger also traverses the turret and elevates and depresses the gun. The turret rotates at 4 rpm. The gunner is also provided with manual controls. An override control similar to the gunner's control but with electrical firing trigger only enables the commander to take over from the gunner if he so desires or if it becomes necessary to do so. There also is an interlock which enables the tank commander to control the 90-mm. gun by aligning it with the cupola machine-gun. And, as in all U.S. tanks, equipment is provided for conducting indirect fire.

It has already been mentioned that the early production vehicles could not be fitted with the cupola in-

The M48A1 tank equipped with the standard fording kit which permitted wading up to a depth of 96 inches. Photo—U.S. Ordnance Corps

The rear view of the M48A2 shows the major redesign of the engine compartment, new louvers, travel lock, pintle and inside telephone box of changed design. Photo—U.S. Ordnance Corps.

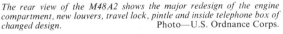

tended. These vehicles had a revolving hatch of the early Sherman type with a hinged cover and a ·50 calibre machine-gun on a cradle. In 1953 an attempt was made to eliminate the coaxial machine-gun, substituting a ·30 calibre machine-gun on a short pedestal mount welded to the turret top to the left of the loader's hatch. However there was interference from the hatch cover preventing all-round fire. A cupola mount with sloping rear and hatch cover hinged at the base was substituted. The ·50 calibre gun mounted in the cupola could be armed, charged and fired from within the turret or fired manually from within the cupola. It had a 200 round ammunition box. A refinement of this cupola was the similar M1 used on the M48A1, A2, A2C and the M67A1. It had five periscopes and a periscopic gun sight and a protruding gun mantlet, but the hatch cover was round and was pivoted on the right instead of being hinged. It used a 100 round ammunition box.

The M1 cupola had 360° traverse. The machine-gun had a range of elevation and depression of +60° and —10°. The gun is mounted with the left side down and is fired electrically. The sight for it is arranged with two settings, one for 500-800 yards and one for 800-1,000 yards. Beyond that range, fire is conducted by means of tracer ammunition. Concentric rings are provided, each of the rings representing a 100 mile per hour lead for anti-aircraft fire although the effectiveness of such fire from any tank is questionable.

The original 10X stereo rangefinder later was replaced by a coincidence type. So many men found themselves unable to use the device and disconnected it that the change was mandatory.

The need for adequate light for night firing resulted in mounting on the gun an 18in. commercial searchlight of 2,000 watts. This light was fitted with electrical shutters which prevented pre- and after-glow. Such lights finally were replaced with Xenon lights which provided infra-red as well as white light. Lights of this kind now are standard on the tanks of practically all nations.

The M48 tanks were able to ford a stream up to a depth of 48 inches. After numerous experiments to simplify the wading equipment which had been developed during World War II, a standard fording kit was developed and issued, permitting fording to a depth of 96 inches. The kit sealed the hull from the entrance of water by means of covers, ducts, hoses, tape and similar means. It also provided a means of escape for engine exhaust gases through the right rear grille door and up and out an exhaust stack. This stack could be jettisoned from within the vehicle by means of release cords. A bilge pump also formed part of the kit. Maximum speed while fording was 4 m.p.h.

HYBRIDS

There are so many variations of the M48 that the best way to keep them straight in one's mind is to list them:

T48, the original T42 chassis with a new turret and hull, 6 bogie wheels and 5 support rollers.

T48E1, numerous modifications.

T48E2, prototype of M48.

T48 with Launcher Kit, six fanned-out smoke launcher kits on each of four turret sides.

M48, original production with early Sherman type cupola and exposed remote control machine-gun and small driver's hatch.

M48 Phase III, M48 with M47 fire control equipment.

M48C, mild steel training tank.

Israeli M48A2 tank during the six day war in 1967.
Photo—Courtesy Tyler Segar

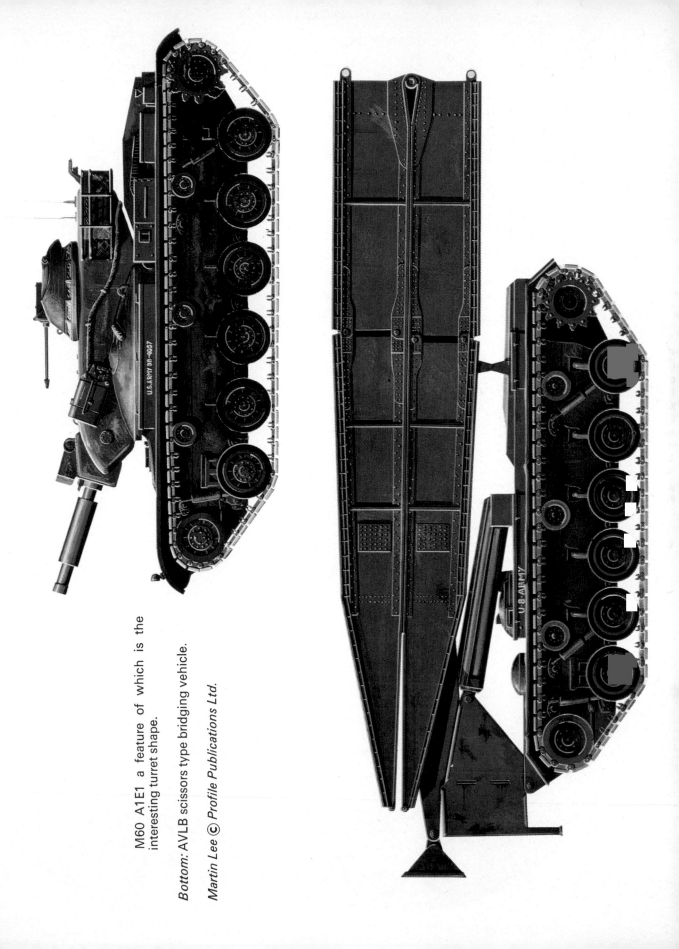

M60 A1E1 a feature of which is the interesting turret shape.

Bottom: AVLB scissors type bridging vehicle.

Martin Lee © Profile Publications Ltd.

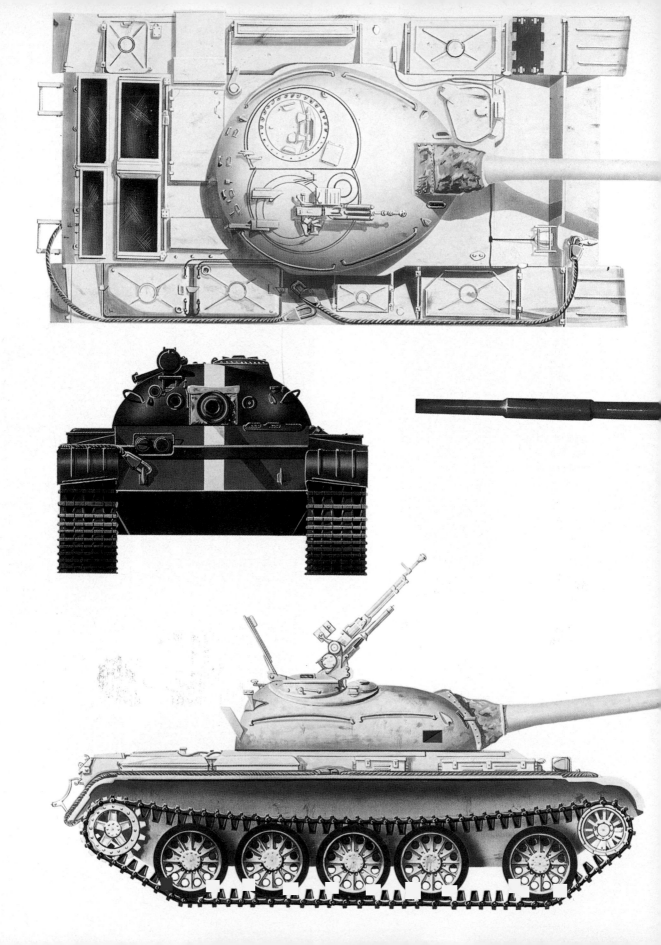

Four views of an early T-54 of the Egyptian Army in the Arab/Israeli War 1967.

Two views (*side/front in dark brown*) Russian T-62 in Prague 1968. The white stripes on turret and hull identified vehicles in the invasion force.

Martin Lee © Profile Publications Ltd.

0 ⊢———————⊣ 4'

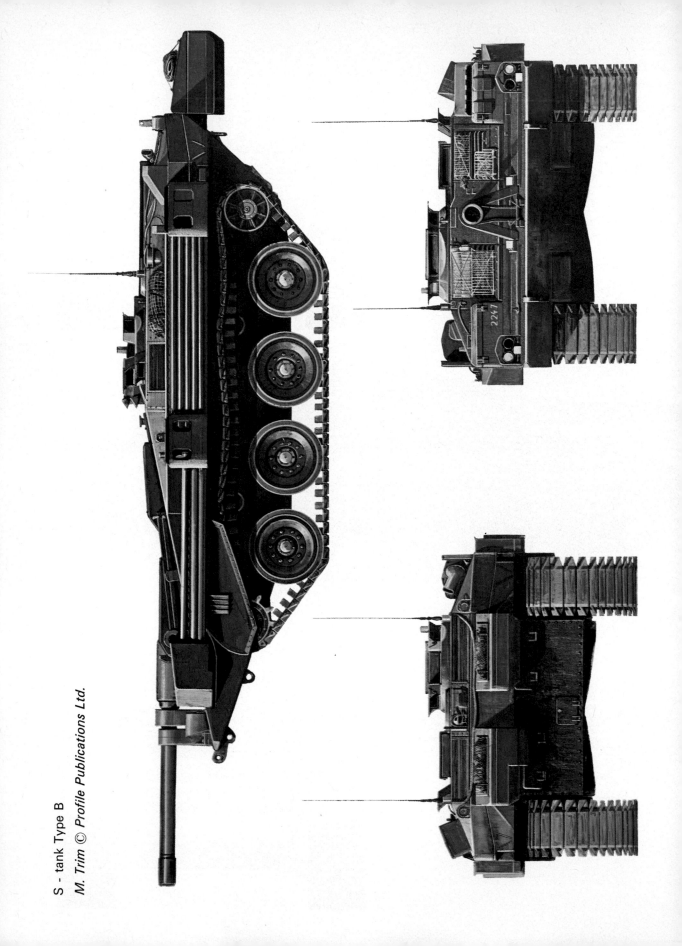

S - tank Type B
M. Trim © Profile Publications Ltd.

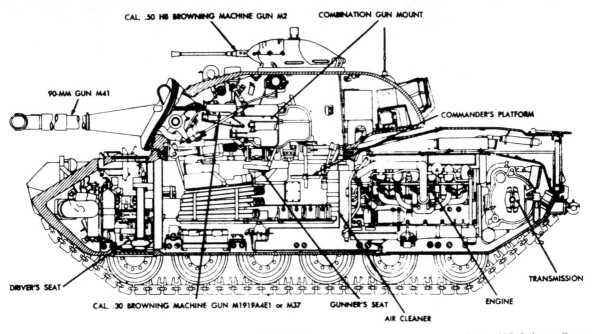

CAL. .50 HB BROWNING MACHINE GUN M2   COMBINATION GUN MOUNT

90-MM GUN M41

COMMANDER'S PLATFORM

DRIVER'S SEAT

TRANSMISSION

CAL. .30 BROWNING MACHINE GUN M1919A4E1 or M37   GUNNER'S SEAT

AIR CLEANER

ENGINE

The differences from the M48 are apparent in this cross-section of the M48A2.

Photo—U.S. Ordnance Corps

M48C with Fender Kits or remote controlled ·30 calibre machine-guns over the tracks.

M48A1, with M1 cupola and large driver's hatch.

M48E1, M48 with British 105-mm. gun, also called M60 Interim Tank.

M48A1E1, M48A1 with British 105-mm. gun.

M48A1E2, diesel engine, No. 2 and No. 4 support rollers removed and M48E2 type compensating idler installed.

M48E2, Prototype of M48A2.

M48A2, diesel engine, later M19 cupola, infra-red equipment, lowered rear doors and rear deck raised 8 inches for better cooling, No. 2 and No. 4 roller removed (except by U.S. Marine Corps), small idler wheel between sprocket and rear bogie removed.

M48A2C, mild steel, prototype M60 type turret.

M48A2E1, M48A2 with multi-fuel engine.

M48A2/SS10, two SS10 missiles right of 90-mm gun, two left, one above.

M48A3, production model of M48A1E2, larger fuel tank, No. 2 and No. 4 support roller reinstated when used in Viet Nam; late production vehicles added a vision block riser between cupola and turret. In Viet Nam, a ·50 calibre MG sometimes was mounted above the cupola and sometimes a 7·62-mm MG with shield was mounted in front of loader's hatch and another MG was substituted in mantlet for the telescopic sight.

M48A4, M48A3 with M60 turret, 105-mm gun and M19 cupola.

M48 with Shillelegh, redesigned turret for 152-mm gun.

M48 with Expendable Roller Mine Clearing Device.

M48 with AGT 1500 Gas Turbine, test rig only.

M48 with Heavy Mine Clearing Roller (High Herman), 25 plain and serrated discs.

An M48A3 in South Vietnam with sandbags on the turret forming a bunker of sorts.
Photo—Courtesy J. W. Loop

M48A3 tanks in South Vietnam as fitted with a vision block ring or vision riser between the commander's cupola and the turret.
Photo—Courtesy J. W. Loop

31

The gunner in the M48A3 has his controls compactly arranged.
Photo—U.S. Army

The M48AVLB was a conventional type of scissors bridgelayer.
Photo—Martin Iger

M48 with Light Mine Clearing Roller (Larrapin' Lou), two units of six serrated discs each.

AVLB, M48 or M48A2 scissors type bridgelayer.

M67 Flame Tank, M48A1 with flame gun replacing the 90-mm. gun.

M67A1, same with tank cupola added.

M67A2, M48A3 with flame gun, three support rollers (except in U.S. Marine Corps).

M88 Tank Recovery Vehicle, ARV with M48 components.

When it became apparent that the 100-mm. L/54 gun on the post-war Soviet tanks was a weapon superior to the 90-mm. L/48 gun of the M48, upgunning of the M48 began as can be seen from the above list. Again, developments elsewhere had forced U.S. designers to follow. During World War II it had been the Germans who continually forced the U.S. to upgun. Now it was the Russians. Since the British and Commonwealth armies as well as those of several of the NATO nations were equipped with the British Centurion tank, it was decided that the successful tests of the Centurion's 105-mm. gun in the M48E1 justified a changeover to that weapon.

THE M60

Thus the M60 armed with the British 105-mm. gun grew out of the M48. In 1960, some 180 were ordered and tested, following which 720 more were ordered. The M60A1 with its longer-nosed turret went into production in 1962. Austria, France, Iran and Italy also received the M60A1. In addition to the 200 furnished to Italy, more were produced there under license even though several European tanks at least its equal were available at the time. The Swedish STRV 103, the French AMX 30 and the German Leopard have better horse-power/weight ratios and far superior silhouettes. With the 105-mm. L/51 gun, the M48A3 is the equal of the M60A1. Unit cost is not greatly different, since the M60A1 cost is stated to be $220,000.

THE SHILLELAGH

At the same time as the British 105-mm. gun was being considered, the U.S. Army established a requirement for future armoured combat vehicles, stating that "a direct fire, armored vehicle-mounted missile . . . be available for operational use at the earliest possible date." The first result of this was the initiation of the Sheridan light reconnaissance vehicle which is not considered by the army to be a tank. It was to be armed with a weapons system known as the Shillelegh. This system was to include the use of a combustible cartridge case which the Army had been working on for a number of years and for which it believed a satisfactory solution had been reached.

The Shillelegh was developed by the Aero-Neutronics Division of Philco-Ford. It is a 152-mm. gun/howitzer capable of firing a conventional projectile as well as a missile. The missile, when fired, is controlled by the gunner who keeps the target in sight through a collimator linked by radio micro-wave acting on the rocket motor nozzle, thus varying the movement of the missile. The gunner must have continuous observation so the gun cannot fire when on the move or at night. It also has the disadvantage which it shares with many other missile systems in that it bathes the

The AVLB scissors type bridging vehicle increased the operating range of its companion M48 and M60 main battletanks.

Photo—Ordnance Magazine

target in IR light before the missile is launched so that it provides early warning through IR energy.

Because it is capable also of firing a conventional projectile the weapon has rather a complicated breech mechanism. The conventional rounds are caseless or rather the cases are combustible, requiring no ejection or disposition. The missile projectile is a solid fuel rocket engine about 44 inches long and weighing about 60 pounds. It has recessed fins which open on firing to stabilize flight. This weapons system adopted for the M551, or Sheridan, was to become the foundation for an improvement also in the main battle tank programme, beginning with the M60A1, converting it into the M60A1E1 and M60A1E2, and also the MBT 70. The last-named was developed jointly with the Republic of Germany (where it is called the Keiler) although the Germans have decided to substitute their own 120-mm. full automatic gun. Unit costs of the MBT 70 rose to about $700,000 and, beginning in 1970, each country

decided to go its own way on this design. The U.S. model was to be simplified, eliminating the variable suspension system, the fire control system and reducing the engine power in order to cut the unit cost to $500,000. The many problems which plagued the programme were due to over-emphasis and misuse of systems analysis techniques. Civilian analyzers apparently evaluated tanks solely as anti-tank weapons which operated as stationary artillery, not taking into consideration the elements of speed, mobility and agility. The full name of this tank is Tank, Combat, Full Tracked, 152-mm. Gun/Launcher, XM 803. Eventually the name of some general will be given to it. But instead of producing the XM 803 in 1970, it was decided to produce the M60A1 with wider tracks for several more years, adding full gun stabilization and improved fire control instrumentation involving solid state electronic computer, laser rangefinder and add-on stabilization. This will make possible the replace-

The M60 AVLB like its M48 predecessor was a conventional type of of scissors bridgelayer.   Photo—Courtesy J. W. Loop

The M60A1 long nose turret provided considerably more interior room than its predecessor turret.   Photo—U.S. Army

The M60 interim tank was the standard M48 modified for installation of the British 105 mm gun.   Photo—U.S. Ordnance Corps

ment of M48 series vehicles still in the hands of both Regular and Reserve units.

The Defense Department originally had intended to adopt the Shillelegh system on a crash basis which would upgun these vehicles until the MBT 70 became available. Modified M60A1 vehicles were to become the M60A1E1 in which an electronic computer replaced the previous mechanical computer. New vehicles produced in the same form were to be called M60A1E2. The first of the former appeared in 1965. The turrets from the modified M60A1 tanks were then to be placed on M48A3 tanks. In the new turret, the gunner and loader are located low on either side of the main armament. The commander is high and to the rear of the gun. The silhouette of the vehicle is low except for the commander's cupola which raises it considerably as is the case with all tanks of the M48-M60 series.

The M60A1E2 tank has night vision devices, a target designating system, laser rangefinder, an electronic

An M60A1 main battle tank being fitted for combat in Vietnam.
Photo—U.S. Army

computer with cant corrector and a target lead sensor. Both the main gun and the commander's gun are stabilized.

The House Armed Service Committee of the Congress noticed in 1967 that, in spite of funds having been appropriated each year, the Army had not deployed these new vehicles. A special investigating subcommittee was created for the purpose of determining the cause of the delay. Production of the M60A1 had been slowed down and finally stopped in 1967 in anticipation of producing the M60A1E2.

The report of the subcommittee was submitted in 1969. It was critical of the programme and its findings received considerable newspaper publicity at the time. However, the report was unfair in that it criticized the entire Shillelegh weapons system whereas the missile handling capacity of the Shillelegh operated extremely well. It was the caseless ammunition for the conventional projectile which caused the problem. It was true that the caseless conventional ammunition developed for the Shillelegh had been considered unsafe by virtue of residue and smoke as early as 1961. By 1964 the effects of humidity which caused misfires and broken rounds had become another problem, followed by another of premature detonation. In 1966, Army Research and Development approved procurement because of a fear of loss of funds in spite of a recommendation to stop procurement until the problems were solved.

Another redesign of the ammunition eliminated the premature detonation problem but the smouldering residue problem continued to be troublesome and dangerous. The weapon itself received an open breech scavenging mechanism using air jets in 1967. In the same year the M60A1E1 turrets were found to have defective hydraulic stabilizers. They could not be mounted but continued to be produced. They were placed in storage while studies continued toward developing a new stabilizer. The scavenger device also was produced before testing and when it became available was found to be dangerous, resulting in slowing the rate of fire. The report went on to describe another redesign of the breech scavenger in 1968. This time it was of the closed breech type.

Some of the new tanks were completed as M60A1 and some were tested with other types of armament. A metal cartridge case was proposed in the same year but it was not adopted because it still was felt that a solution was "just around the corner." The constant optimism and fear of losing funds may have caused a compromise with the original goals but the report was unfair in stating that the result was a weapon lacking any real improvement over existing weapons. The missile firing capability of the Shillelegh is satisfactory and it is to be expected that a solution will be found for the problems of the conventional ammunition even if a return has to be made to cased ammunition.

Some of the Sheridans were sent to Viet Nam. There some problems were found in the considerable shock of firing a heavy weapon in this lighter vehicle, with fouling, with the gun not always returning to battery and with the ammunition which sometimes proved fragile. In general, however, the vehicle and weapon were considered satisfactory by the using service and to have definite potential. The problem of humidity was solved by encasing the rounds in thin plastic in the ammunition racks.

The subcommittee held that the Soviet armour threat was not growing fast enough to justify the actions which had permitted production before development was complete, but General Westmoreland, the Army Chief of Staff, reminded the Armed Services Committee in later testimony that the threat was considered real at the time the decision was made and that it continued to exist. He admitted that the integration of gun, turret and stabilization in the M60A1E2 "proved more difficult" than anticipated.

The result of the hearings was that service testing of the Shillelegh in Viet Nam and at proving grounds undoubtedly will lead to the answers but in the meantime only M60A1 tanks are to be produced. The turrets for the later models will be stored until a final solution is reached.

It would appear that the problems which developed in this and other programs were due to the sub-division of responsibility initiated by the former Secretary of Defense, Robert McNamara, when he caused a complete reorganization of the Defense Department. Prior to that time, the Ordnance Corps developed and the using arm tested and either accepted or rejected the offering. Inter-service rivalry made the system work. The organization later adopted eliminated the Ordnance Corps as a design agency and set up a system which was based on computer-determined "cost-effectiveness" and not only created many more agencies but the agencies apparently were under less control. This was hinted at in another report, this one by the Office of the Controller General.

Weapons developments under the later organization were managed by Project Managers who reported to Army Materiel Command who in turn advised the Assistant Chief of Staff for Force Development who authorized production rather than the Chief of Staff doing so. An over-optimistic Project Manager, or one with the human desire to "look good" so that the Secretary of Defense and the Bureau of the Budget would not be critical from a financial standpoint, could ignore user test reports and submit optimistic reports to higher-ups. Often the reports at higher headquarters were not examined critically and continued to be initialled without question and passed

Project K, the redesigned M60A1 with longer Shillelegh mounted in a new armor plate turret of improved ballistic design.
Photo—Courtesy Defense Operations Division Chrysler Corporation.

M60A1 medium tank with deep water fording kit and commander's tower. Photo—U.S. Army

An M60A1 tank equipped with dozer blade and snorkel indicating a maximum depth of 17 feet which could be forded.
Photo—U.S. Army

The M60A1 as used in Austria shows the change made in the glacis and the simplified supports for the fenders.
Photo—Courtesy Heeres-Film und Lichtbild Stelle

Driver's seat and controls in the M60A1 main battle tank.

Photo—U.S. Army

1. Driver's hatch cover control handle.
2. Periscope M27(3).
3. Brake pressure gage.
4. Tachometer.
5. Periscope, M24.
6. Speedometer.
7. Steering control.
8. Heat diffuser sliding door.
9. Accelerator pedal.
10. Transmission shift lever.
11. Dome light (behind periscope).
12. Auxilliary Power (slaving) receptacles.

13. Control box, interphone.
14. Gage indicator panel.
15. Master control panel.
16. Purge pump handle and heater switch.
17. Headlight assembly stowage bracket.
18. Accelerator locking lever.
19. Seat.
20. Brake pedal.
21. Dimmer switch.
22. Fuel shut-off valve handle.
23. Turret seal hand pump.
24. Turret seal pressure gage.
25. Fixed fire extinguishers.

along. The review by the two agencies bears out this is what happened in the case of the Shillelegh.

As a result of these events, the Defense Department late in 1969 set up what was called PROMAP-70. This was a 300 man task force which began studying the life-cycle costs of new weapons systems in order to develop tighter controls and more realistic cost estimates. One of the first five systems to come under study was the M60A1E2 tank and the Shillelegh missile system. According to *Army* magazine in April, 1970, "the turret stabilization problems which have dogged the M60A1E2 program have now been solved,

permitting modification to get those the Army already has procured into service." Only a limited number will be built because the MBT 70/XM803 is expected to be produced and issued by 1975. The others were completed as M60A1 vehicles.

In addition, the task force stated, as one of its first recommendations, that there should be a better selection of Project Managers initially and that they should be kept on the job longer since the study had shown that 60 per cent of the Project Managers and their staffs had served in such capacities for less than two years.

Loading Shillelegh projectile through loader's hatch in the M60A1E1 medium tank.　　　　Photo—U.S. Army

The opened hatches of this prototype M60A1E2 main battle tank show the ease of access which the vehicle possesses.　　Photo—R. J. Icks

Three-quarter front view of the M60A1E1 shows the unusual turret design, the gun depression limit bar and the crew ladder on the left glacis.
Photo—U.S. Army

This three-quarter rear view of the M60A1E2 shows the vision riser below the cupola and the unusual turret bustle.　　　Photo—U.S. Army

M60A1E2 main battle tank—vision devices are provided for all crew members.

Photo—U.S. Army

THE M60 SERIES

The succession of vehicles in the M60 series can be epitomized as follows:

M60E1, M60 Interim Tank, new long nose turret.

M60E2, driver and driver controls in the turret.

M60A1, improved model, M19 cupola, loader equipped with periscope.

M60A1E1, new turret mounting Shillelegh applied to existing M60A1 tanks.

M60A2 (M66), similar to M60A1 with further turret changes.

M60A1E2, new turret with Shillelegh applied to newly produced M60 tanks.

M60 AVLB, scissors bridgelaying tanks of two different bridge lengths.

T118E1, Armored Engineering Vehicle (Trankdozer), M60A1 chassis with 15 ton crane, A-frame and dozer.

The M88 medium recovery vehicle was based on M48 components and is capable of following main battle tanks into combat if necessary.
Photo—U.S. Ordnance Corps.

The cupola on the M60A1 is the M19, larger than the M1 used on the M48, being four inches higher and nine inches longer. The ·50 calibre machine-gun was electrically fired and charged but the cupola was manually operated. The gun had an elevation of —15° to +60°. This cupola has eight periscopes and the hatch cover was hinged to the rear.

Mention previously was made of the fording kits furnished for the M48 tanks. In the case of the M60, "shore kits" or deep water fording devices have been developed. The vehicles are sealed as before, but in addition a high cylinder is provided for the commander so that the vehicle can be completely submerged, the driver then being controlled by the commander through an interphone. This snorkel is a device similar to that in use in a number of armies today, most of them differing in detail only. With it the M60 can ford up to a depth of 15 feet.

A new device considered for adoption on the later tanks is a blade antenna for the radios. The success of this type of antenna in helicopters led to its test on tanks. Its low silhouette eliminates a hazard when the vehicle is near power lines but the principal advantage is that it provides much sharper tuning and therefore much better reception.

In addition to the normal radios that can be carried, there is available the VRC-24, a special radio with a short cylindrical antenna for using the tactical aircraft radio network.

The Chrysler Corporation in 1970 offered commercially a variation of the M60A1 which was known as Project K. This is a version which compared favourably with the M60A1E2. The armament is a stabilized longer barrelled Shillelegh with coaxial 7·62-mm. M73 machine-gun and equipped with a three round loader's assist device in a new ballistically well-shaped low silhouette plate armour turret with new vision cupola and remote controlled 50 calibre machine-gun. Ammunition stowage was raised to 57/7600/1530 rounds. Suspension changes included doubling the number of torsion bars, substituting rotary hydraulic shock absorbers which replaced the previous friction snubbers and substituting a new aluminium body track with detachable pads. These changes permit bogie wheel movement to be increased from 12·3 in. to 17·8 in., making possible an improvement in both speed and cross-country ability. Total weight of the vehicle increased somewhat less than one short ton.

TANK NUMBERING SYSTEM

As might be expected there is a system for numbering vehicles in the U.S. Army but, even though a single system is provided for in regulations, liberties seem to be taken with it because numbers appearing on vehicles in photographs occasionally do not appear to follow the system.

Since 1954, all vehicle numbers have been centrally controlled and consist of a combination of letters and numbers, excluding the letters I, O and Q. The number for each vehicle is supposed to comprise a uniform length of six places. The first numerals designate the type. This is followed by a letter or letters singly going through the alphabet and then double letters going through the alphabet again. Finally there is a number within the particular letter group.

Tanks and armoured recovery vehicles have the prefix 09; cargo vehicles (except amphibious) are 11; self-propelled guns, armoured personnel carriers and armoured utility vehicles are 12; while armoured cars, amphibious cargo carriers, half tracks and LVTs are 13. In interpreting the regulation, however, the zero (zed) sometimes is omitted before the 9 in the case of tanks, thus adding another digit to the number following the letter or letters.

References

Army Times. Armor. Ordnance.

Armor in Viet Nam, ARMOR COMMAND ADVISORY DETACHMENT, *Saigon, 1966.*

Design and Development of Fighting Vehicles, R. M. OGORKIEWICZ, *Doubleday & Company, Inc., Garden City, 1968.*

Die Panzerwaffe, PANZERTRUPPENSCHULE, *Zwoelfaxing, 1964.*

Hearings on Military Posture Before Committee on Armed Services, House of Representatives, 91st Congress, 1st Session, HASC no. 91-14, *Government Printing Office, Washington, 1969.*

History and Role of Armor, U.S. ARMY ARMOR SCHOOL, *Fort Knox, 1968 and 1970 editions.*

M48 90 mm. Gun Tank, FM 17-79, DEPARTMENT OF THE ARMY, *Washington, 1955.*

Kampfpanzer 1916-1966, F. M. VON SENGER UND ETTERLIN, *J. F. Lehmanns Verlag, Munich, 1966.*

Panzerkennblaetter, FRITZ WIENER UND HERBERT HAHN, *Vienna, 1957-1961.*

The flame gun on the M67 flame tank was a close replica of the 90-mm. gun on the standard tank.   Photo—Chemical Warfare Service

Project K, DEFENSE OPERATIONS DIVISION, *Chrysler Corporation, Detroit, 1970.*

Review of Army Tank Program, Report of Armed Services Investigating Subcommittee, Armed Services Committee, 91st Congress, HR 105, *Government Printing Office, Washington, 1969.*

Review of Development and Procurement of New Combat and Tactical Vehicle by the Department of the Army, Report to the Congress of the United States by the Controller General of the United States, *General Accounting Office, Washington, 1960.*

Report to the Congress—Need for Management Improvement in Expediting Development of Major Weapon Systems Satisfactory for Combat Use, *General Accounting Office, Washington, 1969.*

Swift Sword, S. L. A. MARSHALL, *American Heritage Publishing Company, New York, 1967.*

Supplies and Equipment—Registration of Motor Vehicles, AR 700-10 and Changes 1, DEPARTMENT OF THE ARMY, *Washington, 1954-1959.*

Twenty-Two Fateful Days, D. R. MANKEKAR, *Manaktaton, Bombay, 1966.*

The World's Armoured Fighting Vehicles, F. M. VON SENGER UND ETTERLIN, *Translated by R. M. Ogorkiewicz, Macdonald, London, 1960.*

Weapon Mounts for Secondary Armament, Prepared for Detroit Arsenal by G. O. NOVILLE & ASSOCIATES INC., *Reference No. 206, Los Angeles, 1957.*

The T118E1 Armoured Engineer Vehicle was a general purpose vehicle armed with a 165-mm. assault gun.   Photo: Courtesy J. W. Loop

DATA COMPARISON CHART FOR THE BASIC VEHICLES IN THE M48-M60 SERIES

Item	M48, M48C	M48A1	M48A2, A2C	M48A3	M60	M60A1	M60A1E1, E2	M67 USMC	M67A1 US Army
Crew	4	4	4	4	4	4	4	3	3
Length									
Travel	292 15/16"	289 15/16"	292¾"	292¾"	320"	325"	275½	274⅜"	271⅛"
Gun F'w'd	332 9/16"	343 23/32"	342"	342"	366½"	371½"	288¾"	324¼"	320⅜"
Vehicle	264"	270½"	270⅝"	293"	273½"	273½"	275½"	274⅜"	270½"
Width	148"	143"	143"	143"	143"	143"	143"	143"	143"
Height									
O/A	127⅝"	123 5/16"	121⅝"	123" (A)	126½"	128¼"	130⅜"	121⅝"	121⅝"
Vehicle	107½"	123 5/16	121⅝"	123"	126½"	118"	130⅜"	121⅝"	121⅝"
Armament									
Main	90mm. L/48	90mm. L/48	90mm. L/48	90mm. L/48	105mm. L/51	105mm. L/51	152mm.	M7-6 F/T	M7A1-6 F/T
Coax	·30 Cal	·30 Cal	·30 Cal	·30 Cal	7·62mm.	7·62mm.	7·62mm.	·30 Cal	·30 Cal
AA	·50 Cal	·50 Cal	·50 Cal	·50 Cal	·50 Cal	·50 Cal	12·7mm.	·50 Cal	·50 Cal
Ammo (Rds)									
90mm.	60	60	64	62	57	60*	46	380 gals	380 gals
·30 Cal	5900	5900	5950	6000	5000	5000*	5500	3500	3500
·50 Cal	180	500	1365	630	846	500*	900	660	660
Armour*									
Tracks***									
Width									
Pitch									
Shoes	79	79	79	79	81	81		79	79
Weight (Pds)									
Combat	99,000	104,000	104,000	104,000	102,000	106,000	113,500	104,790	105,790
Empty	93,125	97,000	97,000	98,000	95,300	97,000	97,000	99,975	100,975
Road Wheels	6	6	6	6	6	6	6	6	6
Support Wheels	5	5	3	3-5	3	3-5	3	5	3
Clearance	15½"	15½"	15¼"	16"	16"	16"	18"	15¼"	15¼"
Grd Pressure	11·2	11·8	11·9	11·8	11·1	11·3	12·2	11·9	12·0
Electrical	24v	24v	24v	24v	24v	24v	24v	24v	24v
Fuel (US Gals)	200	200	335	375	375	375	—	200	335
Engine	AV 1790-5B, 7, 7B, 7C	7C	7C	2A	2	2A	2A	7	8
Transmission	CD 850-4, 4A, 4B	4B	5	6	6	6A	6A	6	6
Speeds	2F2R	2F2R	2F2R	2F2R	2F2R	2F2R	2F2R	2F2R	2F2R
HP/rpm	810/2800	810/2800	810/2800	865/2800	750/2400	—	—	810/2800	—
Traverse	Man/Mech	—	Man/Hydr	—	—	—	—	Man/Mech	Man/Hydr
Vehicle Speed	26 m.p.h.	26	30	30	30	30	30	26	30
Radius (Miles)	70	70	160	288	310	310	370	160	160
Remarks	Small Driver Hatch	Large Driver Hatch	Large	Large	Large	Large	—	—	—

ALL
Grade 60 per cent.

Turn Pivot

Ford 48"****

Trench 102"

Climb 36"

Radio Various

* Later 63/5500/900 Rounds
** All 25-110 mm.
*** All 28" wide, 6 15/16" pitch
**** Ford 96" with Snorkel
(A) About 130" with vision ring

The MBT 70 tank is fitted with a different version of the Shillelegh
Photo: Courtesy Allison Division General Motor Corporation

Chieftain.

(Army PR)

Chieftain and Leopard Main Battle Tanks

A TANK has three main attributes: firepower, mobility and protection. Few would dispute the primacy of firepower to defeat enemy armour and provide direct fire support for other arms, although the maximum range needed for the former rôle is a matter of some controversy in itself. But it is over the best way of ensuring the survival of the tank that views tend to diverge most sharply. The British represent one school of thought which contends that protection is best ensured by armouring the vehicle to such an extent that it can absorb punishment from the majority of enemy weapons and enable it to manoeuvre or close with the enemy with relative immunity: tactical mobility can then take third place. This concept is hotly contested by the opposing school, the Germans being prominent members, which considers that so many weapons on the battlefield are capable of defeating the thickest armour at normal combat ranges that it is not worth protecting above a certain minimum level while a lower weight permits a freedom of manoeuvre and agility that more than makes up for the relegation of passive protection to third position.

Two modern tanks exemplify these different viewpoints, the British Chieftain and the German Leopard Standardpanzer.

DEVELOPMENT HISTORIES
CHIEFTAIN MAIN BATTLE TANK (FV 4201)

Conceived in 1943 to obtain a superiority over German tanks that had been almost completely lacking until then, the Centurion Medium Gun Tank first saw action in the completely different conditions of the Korean war, and in that same year, 1951, the General Staff in London started to plan for Medium Gun Tank

No. 2 (Medium Gun Tank No. 1 being FV 221 Caernarvon). It was reasoned that while the Russian T-34/85 was still a threat (as it proved initially in Korea) it was out-matched by Centurion and that a successor, probably with a more powerful gun, must be nearing service. The now familiar warning against never knowingly being under-gunned was reiterated and a number of guide-lines were set out. As production of Centurion was then due to end in 1954, and that of Conqueror in 1957, it was suggested tentatively that the new tank could be available not long after this latter date. A maximum weight limit of 67 long tons was stipulated although it was hastily added that 45 tons should be possible. No increase of road speed over that of Centurion was looked for although the desired power to weight ratio of 20:1 indicated that acceleration and agility were to be more important than previously and an average cross country speed of 15 m.p.h. was asked for. Up to 80 main armament rounds were desirable, although 60 would be accepted, stabilisation of the weapon system was to be incorporated if it proved successful on Centurion (it did), a maximum rate of fire of 10 rounds per minute was specified together with a capability for aimed fire up to 1,000 yards by night. MGT No. 2 was also to be able to swim.

A study based on these criteria at Fighting Vehicles Research and Development Establishment (FVRDE) was completed in July 1951. A 105 mm. high velocity gun of U.S. origin was mounted on the top of a cleft turret, and as the gun was both longer and heavier than the current British 20-pdr. (84 mm.), it was suspended well to the rear in order to keep its point of balance as close to the centre of the suspension as possible. The breech was outside the turret ring as a

Above and below: *A Chieftain Mark 2* (right) *and a pre-production Leopard together for comparative trials.*   (FVRDE, CCR)

result and an automatic loader had to be provided, operated remotely. A combat weight of 48 tons was postulated even when priority in protection was given to the crew rather than components and only 40 rounds were stowed, although a saving in space and weight would have been likely if the driver was moved into the turret. The running gear was to be modelled on the modified Horstmann system and resilient road wheels used in the FV 200 series (see Conqueror *Profile*) but there were to be no top rollers. The scheme was eventually dropped when it became clear that both the gun and its fixed ammunition were imposing unacceptable weight penalties. A joint investigation with the Armament Research and Development Establishment was then set in train to look into the possibility of using liquid propellant, but this too was discontinued in favour of research into the further development of the principle of using bagged propellant charges—not with the usual screw-type breech block—but a sliding block with obturation being obtained by an expanding steel ring, a method that had first been applied in the German 150 mm. medium howitzer 18/43 in World War II. Consultations with the Royal Navy also showed that bag charges were no more vulnerable than those enclosed in metal cases, as there is a significant pause between strike and ignition that will usually pass un-noticed in the latter container, and the possibility was mooted of

having storage bins with vents direct to atmosphere in case of a fire.

In 1954 the General Staff made it clear that the replacement for Centurion must have a more effective gun and armour with an automotive performance at least as good but, in the event, Centurion itself partially met these demands when it was up-gunned to 105 mm. and its protection improved. Up to then this calibre gun was the largest that could be mounted economically with an adequate number of rounds in a vehicle whose weight was limited to 100,000 pounds, but a thorough assessment was started that year to determine the optimum calibre for a tank gun to meet future N.A.T.O. requirements as the bagged charge system appeared to be significantly lighter than a more conventional one of the same calibre. A figure of 120 mm. was arrived at and a gun of this calibre was installed in a new design of vehicle whose driver reclined in the closed-down position, it being his sitting height that largely determines the height of the tank hull, and any reduction in that is a potential saving in weight. In mid-1954 a new V-8 engine was proposed to replace the veteran Meteor, the auxiliary generating engine being mounted in the Vee, together with an automatic transmission. The estimated combat weight of this vehicle was in the region of 47 tons although it was hoped to reduce this by two tons at least.

Above and below: *A small scale model of an early design for FV 4201 Medium Gun Tank No. 2. Note the similarity of the turret design to that on FV 214 Conqueror and the complex sloping of the glacis plate.* (FVRDE, CCR)

Leyland Motors had been nominated as the main design contractors for the new FV 4201 and they now started work, although they were still heavily involved at this time in the development of the Centurions 7 and 8. The first visible result was the appearance of FV 4202—the "40-ton Centurion"—which appeared in early 1956 to prove the feasibility of the driver's reclining position and a new design of turret which dispensed with the need for a mantlet. The development process was then slowed somewhat by a decision on the part of the United Kingdom and the United States to make certain assemblies interchangeable on their respective tanks and after a great deal of redesigning this was achieved for the turrets of FV 4201

and T95*. A further delay was caused by the N.A.T.O. decision in 1957 that fighting vehicles should have engines capable of running on a wide variety of fuels: the multi-fuel policy. This now necessitated a change of engine for FV 4201 and a German compression ignition

*T95 weighed 32 tons and included a number of innovations, among them being a smooth bore 90-mm. gun (later replaced by the 152-mm. gun/launcher used on M551 Sheridan and proposed for MBT 70), a hydro-pneumatic suspension which could be used to vary the vehicle's height as well as a gas turbine power plant. Visually similar to the Soviet T-54 and Japan's new ST-B the concept was eventually abandoned in favour of the more conventional M60.

Above and below: *FV 4202; the so-called 40-ton Centurion built by Leyland Motors to provide practical experience of a number of concepts intended for FV 4201, including the reclining position for the driver and the mantlet-less turret.* (FVRDE, CCR)

design was chosen for further development by Leylands under the designation of L60. The two-stroke, vertically opposed piston layout was favoured on the grounds that, not only did it give the best configuration for multi-fuel applications, but it was also easy to service, had few moving parts, low bearing loads and had good cold starting characteristics. Unfortunately its installation involved the complete redesign of the power compartment and another ton was added to the all-up weight which was now in the region of 50 tons.

The General Staff finally issued the military characteristics for FV 4201 on August 21, 1958 as a detailed guide to the attributes and performance required by the User. It was prefaced by a brief statement setting out the guiding principles which were to govern its design, whose chief characteristic was to be its highly effective gun/armour combination, followed by agility and a capacity for sustained action. In noting the need to start the destruction of enemy

armour at the longest possible range, and withstand attack by medium artillery (a lesson learned in Korea), as well as from other weapons when closing with the enemy, a number of important increases in specification were demanded. Among these was a larger arc of elevation for the main armament, as the 7° or 8° depression available on Conqueror had proved inadequate to enable it to take up acceptable defensive fire positions, and more frontal protection. A rate of fire of ten rounds per minute for the first minute and six in each of the subsequent four minutes was also called for. An increase in the top speed to not less than 26 m.p.h. and a desirable radius of action of 300 miles at 15 miles in the hour also represented important increments in performance made necessary by the dispersion of forces on the nuclear battlefield. Yet, together with the addition of a number of other facilities, the tank's all-up weight was still not to exceed 45 tons, although this figure had reluctantly to be relaxed later to 116,000 pounds (51·8 tons) as

One of the first prototypes of Chieftain having the original low suspension. (FVRDE, CCR)

Prototype P5 completed in early 1962. Note the thermal sleeve fitted on the 120-mm. gun barrel. (FVRDE, CCR)

A line up, from left to right, of a Conqueror Mark 2, a Centurion Mark 7/1 and an early prototype of Chieftain. (FVRDE, CCR)

insistence on the earlier figure would have resulted in unacceptable delays to the project pending further research and development.

Detailed design at Leylands really got under way in 1958 but in August that year Vickers-Armstrong at Newcastle were brought in to take over responsibility for the turret and installation of the weapons. Development of the L60 engine was being pushed forward meanwhile at Leylands and Rootes and it was decided to adopt the TN12 semi-automatic "hot-shift" gearbox that had been designed originally for the defunct FV 300 light tank series.

In the specification for the meeting convened in March 1959 to accept the design of the mock-up, the all-up weight was quoted as being around 100,000 pounds, the height to the turret roof 7 ft. 10 in., a hull length of 22 ft. 3 in., a ground clearance of 17 in., 60 rounds of 120 mm. ammunition, 250 imperial gallons of fuel, the engine developing 700 b.h.p. at a crank-shaft speed of 2,400 r.p.m. and a power-to-weight ratio that had decreased to 15·5 b.h.p./ton. Among other features that were subsequently to change as development progressed, the gunner laid the armament by a peri-binocular sight with injected graticules, tangent elevation being applied automatically by cams appropriate to the nature of ammunition selected. The User accepted the mock-up in principle although the large number of modifications asked for involved structural alterations to both hull and turret designs.

The first prototype P1 was completed in September 1959 and incorporated a low-power L60 engine, the weight of the turret being simulated by a circular superstructure, and six more prototypes were delivered for troop trials between July 1961 and April 1962, production being shared equally by Vickers-Armstrong and the Royal Ordnance Factory at Leeds. Extensive automotive trials were being carried out meanwhile and a number of defects became apparent

An early prototype showing its paces during a demonstration in August 1963. The cupola hatches are in the "umbrella" position to give the commander some degree of overhead protection and a better field of view than was possible with the early design of vision devices. (Keystone)

A prototype prepared for troop trials. Note the changes in the cupola assembly and the stowage racks on the rear of the turret. (FVRDE, CCR)

An early prototype negotiating a rough test track at FVRDE. The dummy bin on the front of the glacis plate and the cover on the nose of the turret were fitted during the first public appearance of the vehicle. (Keystone)

A prototype Chieftain starting a hill climb. One of the rear turret stowage racks has been replaced by part of the ventilation equipment, the exhaust system is still in the development stage and the light projector is not fitted. (FVRDE, CCR)

Mark 1 Chieftain. The external components of the ventilation equipment are fitted and a new stowage rack has been fitted on to the left rear of the turret. The split covers on the commander's cupola are open. None of the comparatively few Mark 1 versions was issued to the Service. (CCR)

in the engine, caused mainly by excessive vibration. While these were cured by fitting dampers on the crankshaft their addition involved the lengthening of the hull. Overheating in the gearbox was overcome by increasing the oil flow in conjunction with the addition of a heat exchanger but these changes involved moving the exhaust silencers outside the hull structure into an armoured box bolted on the rear as well as increasing the size of the deck louvres. All these modifications added weight, which had by now risen to 49·5 tons in the prototypes, and as the running gear had been designed to the original limit of 45 tons, this too had to be strengthened. The need to limit damage to roads during exercises in Germany led to the addition of rubber pads on the tracks and raised the weight by a further 1,000 pounds. It was also found that the nominal ground clearance of 17 in. specified originally was too small and it was increased to 22 in. by fitting the same diameter road wheels that had been used for Centurion and raising the track adjusting wheel and final drive assemblies. This modification was achieved, however, at the expense of an increase in the overall height of only one inch.

Firing trials of the new L11 120 mm. mounted in the turret started in 1961 and proved very satisfactory, although the User asked for a number of changes in the commander's vision cupola for the Mark 2 version of what was now known as Chieftain Main Battle Tank. Forty vehicles were built to the Mark 1 specification, whose chief visible difference from the Mark 2 is the split hatch in the commander's cupola—similar to that used in Centurion Marks 8, 10 and 13—whereas the Mark 2 has a single hatch cover. The rear of the turret was also redesigned for this mark to incorporate CBR filtration and ventilation units and a number of detailed changes were made to the interior. A weight reduction exercise involved a slight reduction in the number of rounds stowed and modifications to the protection specification involved, *inter alia,* the armour on the light projector being removed. The rigid panel design of flotation equipment was also replaced by a schnorkel deep wading kit.

Some of the first Mark 1 tanks had been issued meanwhile to the 1st and 5th Royal Tank Regiments in Germany for troop trials, the design was accepted for service on May 1, 1963 and delivery of the first vehicles built to the production specification was made to the 11th Hussars in Germany in early 1967. The first Mark 3—incorporating an improved auxiliary generator, modifications to the main engine to increase its reliability, better stowage and a new commander's cupola—was delivered in September 1969 and weighs 53 long tons. The Mark3/3 will have further improvements to its automotive systems and to its range finding performance. In mid-1970 the Mark 5 was announced with its engine uprated to 750 b.h.p. and having a combat weight of 54 tons.

The development history of Chieftain clearly shows some of the influences that act and inter-act if the User is to get what he wants. Compromises will always be

Leopard (right) with combat carrier. (German MOD)

A prototype modified with the raised suspension system and incorporating the armoured cover for the exhausts.
(FVRDE, CCR)

Mark 2 negotiating a minor obstacle during a demonstration. This tank has the much-improved commander's cupola and the new hatch cover is apparent.
(FVRDE, CCR)

The new periscopes in the commander's cupola and changes to the stowage on the turret are shown in this Mark 2.
(FVRDE, CCR)

Mark 2 Chieftain moving at speed across rough ground.
(FVRDE, CCR)

necessary as the requirements of firepower, protection and mobility are incompatible to a greater or lesser extent, regardless of the order of priority in which they are placed. But the length of time needed to bring a tank into service, especially in peacetime when the capital investment, development and industrial resources have to be won at the expense of more profitable civilian projects, force the User to forecast who and where the enemy will be, and how equipped, at least 15 years hence if the tank is not to be obsolescent when it arrives in service. The designer, for his part, has not only to compete with the changing views of the User but also must make his own forecasts to ensure that the engineering techniques and materials used are the best available when production starts, no mean task in an era when the growth of knowledge in these fields is almost exponential. Again, he must

ensure that his design is capable of continuing development after the tank is actually in service to maintain its relevance to the tactical doctrine of the time: the history of Centurion and the modern Soviet Mediums illustrates this well. Production and logistic economics also dictate the desirability for standardizing designs on an international basis and this will usually entail the reconciliation, not only of the capabilities required, but also of differing engineering techniques. This was apparent in the development of Chieftain but even more so in the case of Leopard. With these factors in mind the development of the latter can be traced somewhat more briefly, although this by no means implies that it was necessarily less eventful than that for Chieftain, as a comparison of the original specification for the "European" tank with that for the production Standardpanzer will indicate.

Three views of a Chieftain and basic dimensions.

(COI)

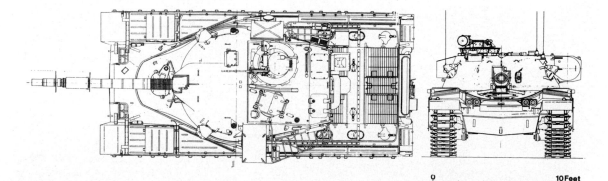

OVERALL DIMENSIONS

Height (commander's spot light)	115·9 ins.
Length with gun forward	424·6 ins.
Length with gun stowed	384·2 ins.
Width over skirting plates	137·6 ins.
Width (including searchlight)	142·5 ins.
Track centres	107·0 ins.
Width of track shoes	24·0 ins.

0   10 Feet

Small scale model of the Porsche KG (Group A) design to the original tripartite specification. Although the Rheinmetall 105-mm. gun is installed the design of the tank as a whole bears a remarkable resemblance to the Standardpanzer in production.

The mockup for the Warneke Group B concept which was automotively the more advanced of the two although they both shared the common Type I turret.

Group A prototype I in 1961.   (Soldat und Technik)

Prototype I of Group A mounting the British 105-mm. L7 gun. The driver's compartment had to be moved subsequently to the other side of the hull to make way for ammunition stowage for the gun which is loaded from the left.   (Soldat und Technik)

Standardpanzer Prototype I from Group B.
(Soldat und Technik)

(Soldat und Technik)

LEOPARD STANDARDPANZER

The Bundeswehr was equipped on formation with a large number of American M47 Patton tanks which had the advantage of being very cheap and available in quantity. But their design was also old and somewhat unsatisfactory, and although the Bundeswehr had a number of the later M48A2 models, it seemed clear that the U.S. philosophy of tank design was not altogether compatible with German tactical ideas: a combat weight of the order of 50 tons was definitely thought to be too high, for example. This view was also shared by France and Italy, both of whom had also been equipped with M47s, and the three nations agreed to formulate jointly the military characteristics for a new European tank. Germany was especially anxious to build up her own armament industry again in order to take a greater share in international projects where the skills and efficiency of

her heavy industry could be used to the best advantage.

The outline specification that emerged in 1957 called for a 30 metric (29·5 long) ton vehicle having a multi-fuel air-cooled engine, a power to weight ratio of 30 b.h.p./ton, a radius of action of 220 miles, an advanced torsion bar or hydro-pneumatic suspension, a maximum ground pressure of 11·3 lb./sq. in., its overall height not to exceed 7 ft. 2 in. nor its width 10 ft. 4 in. The gun was to be capable of defeating 150 mm. of armour sloped at 60° and a maximum range of 2,500 metres was envisaged. The ammunition capacity was not to be less than that for current American tanks and immunity was specified against 20 mm. rounds fired at short range. These parameters were strongly influenced by three main considerations: the need for excellent acceleration and agility across country, the results of a study which showed that the carrying capacity of bridges in Central Europe was predominantly in the 30 to 40 ton bracket and,

Top right and below: *Prototype type IIA with the cross turret rangefinder removed in favour of the 0·5-in. ranging gun.*
(German MOD)

lastly, the view that development of kinetic and chemical energy ammunition had reached such a peak of efficiency that passive protection against them was subject to sharply diminishing returns in terms of combat efficiency. Agility was preferable to armour.

The defence ministries in France and Germany then authorized the construction of two prototypes from the state-owned Atelier de Construction d'Issy-les-Moulineaux (AMX) and from each of two German consortia. The forming of a consortium for a specific project is typical of the German approach in international development (it has been used subsequently in the case of the MBT 70 and a number of aerospace projects), and here consisted of Group A under the leadership of Porsche KG* and Group B under the Warneke office of Ruhrstahl. The contract for the development of a common turret was awarded to Rheinmetall GmbH. The two vehicles from Group A were delivered for trials in January 1961 and those from Group B in the following September. Both designs were similar in appearance but that from

Porsche was slightly longer, heavier and better protected although both had started the almost inexorable climb in all-up weight, the Porsche having reached 32·5 tons. Both used the Daimler Benz 838 engine in the interests of standardizing on a basic design that was to be used in the lighter AFVs, and the parallel development of a two-stroke series by Rheinstahl-Hanomag was abandoned accordingly. Despite their outward similarity, however, the Warneke design was technically the more advanced, notably in its running gear which was to have a hydropneumatic system combining springing with shock absorption and the vehicle could be raised or lowered by altering the volume of oil in the cylinders. The alternative Dubonnet scheme regulated the distribution of the running load over the individual road wheels. The transmission was also of a more advanced design. Of the two turrets one mounted Rheinmetall's own 105 mm. gun in conjunction with an optical range-finder under the gunner's control and the other had the British L7 gun of the same calibre that had been selected for the Centurion, M60, the Vickers Battle Tank and the Swiss Pz 61. The British 0·50 in. ranging gun was also installed in this turret.

As a result of trilateral trials in Germany later in 1961 a number of changes to the specification were agreed, among them being a wading capability to a

---

*Professor F. Porsche was head of the Tank Commission until he was dismissed in 1943 after differences of opinion with Speer, although he continued to work as a consultant. The 185-ton Maus heavy tank project was under his general direction.

The first Leopard to quantity production standards leaving the line at Krauss-Maffei AG in September 1965, watched by the then Minister of Defence Herr von Hassel.
(Deutsche Presse-Agentur)

Above and below: *Leopards on manoeuvres.*
(Krauss-Maffei and German MOD)

Above and middle left: *A Prototype IIA. Note the vertical louvres in the exhaust grille and the 7·62-mm. MG1 on the turret roof.*
(Soldat und Technik)

Prototype IIA Leopards at the first public demonstration in July 1963. Note the re-positioning of the driver's compartment.
(Associated Press)

Prototype II Leopards during troop trials at the Panzertruppenschule II Münsterlager.

depth of 26 ft.* although the need to keep the weight within the original limit was reiterated. The first outwardly apparent split in the agreement arose in the following year when the French decided on the development of their own 105 mm. gun whose only tank-killing ammunition is a spin-stabilized HEAT round while the Germans preferred to have the three types of attack available with the British gun (APDS, HESH and the American HEAT)† as well as being attracted by the lower unit costs and standardization of logistical support within the N.A.T.O. alliance. The Group B automotive design was also abandoned as a result of evaluating a further 26 prototypes from Group A and four from Group B as it was clear that the complexity of the latter would result in delays into service. These 26 Group IIA tanks were sent to a special trials unit, the Panzerlehrbataillon 93 at the Münster Lager Panzertruppenschule II in the autumn of 1962 where the design became known as Leopard. The ranging gun was abandoned as a result of these trials in favour of the longer ranging capability of an optical instrument.

Above and below: Prototype II Leopards during troop trials at the Panzertruppenschule II Münsterlager.

*As it had been for Maus. The requirement was later relaxed for Leopard to 16·5 ft.
†APDS=armour-piercing, discarding-sabot. HESH=high-explosive, squash-head. HEAT=high-explosive, anti-tank.

A IA prototype compared with an M48A2 tank.
(Soldat und Technik)

Preproduction versions of Leopard and AMX 30 during comparative trials.
(Soldat und Technik)

Above and below: *Preproduction Leopard with Turret III. Note the reinstatement of the cross-turret rangefinder, the modified arrangements of the turret stowage racks to allow access to the ammunition loading hatch as well as the now horizontal louvres in the exhaust grilles.*
(German Army official)

Above and below: *Preproduction version of Leopard with the commander's panoramic periscope installed.* (RAC Centre)

Above and below: *Preproduction Standardpanzer with Series III turret.* (German MOD)

Left: *Preproduction version of Leopard with the commander's panoramic periscope installed and a coaxially-mounted IR searchlight on the centre of the mantlet.* (RAC Centre)

Preproduction Leopard with turret III.

Preproduction Standardpanzer with Series III turret.
(German MOD)

The final decision to develop a purely German design was taken in mid-1963 and procurement for the Bundeswehr was authorized in July. Apart from purely technical differences—which were fundamental enough in themselves—it seems that the decision was precipitated by a change in French defence policy so that funds for producing the new tank would not be available until 1965, whereas the replacement of the Bundeswehr's ageing M47s was becoming increasingly urgent. Krauss-Maffei AG of Munich was appointed as main contractor for the series, having considerable experience in tank manufacture, and the first Leopard left the production line on September 9, 1965, its combat weight having risen a full ten tons among many other changes to the original specification. A purely technical comparison in August and September 1963 had shown, however, that despite this increase in weight the Leopard was markedly more agile than the French version (AMX 30) and the L7 gun was judged to be the more effective. The original tripartite agreement finally disintegrated when the Italians decided to adopt the American M60 which they would build under licence, although they later agreed to procure the Leopard.

The order for 1,845 Leopards for the Bundeswehr was completed in 1968 but orders for 334 from Belgium, 78 for Norway, 415 for the Netherlands and 800 for Italy have prolonged the production run subsequently. Spain has also expressed interest in procuring this tank. At the beginning of June 1970 the total number of Leopards supplied and on order was 3,500—excluding the recovery and engineer versions.

The cancellation of the joint MBT-70 project with the U.S.A. has left the Bundeswehr without a replacement for the obsolescent M48 tanks and a much improved Mark 2 version of Leopard is planned for production in 1975.

Panzerbataillon 83 at Lüneberg, the first service unit to be equipped with Leopard, parading in March 1966. (DPA)

Production versions of Leopard. Among the number of changes visible note the moving of the smaller searchlight to the left of the mantlet to avoid back-scatter of light into the sights.

(Soldat und Technik)

A production Leopard on a road march.   (German MOD)

CHIEFTAIN AND LEOPARD DESCRIBED

BOTH the Chieftain and the Leopard are conventional in layout with the driver in the forward part of the hull, the fighting compartment and turret in the centre and the power plant and transmission at the rear. The glacis on Chieftain consists of a cast armoured plate at a high obliquity and is faired into the fabricated hull walls in a way that is reminiscent of the Soviet IS-2 (KV and IS *Profile*) where, too, the driver sat in the centre. The diameter of the turret ring is such that panniers are required to carry it over the tracks either side and these panniers extend rearwards alongside the engine and transmission compartments and contain fillers for the bag-type fuel tanks. A resilient rail round the engine covers prevents metal-to-metal contact when the 120-mm. gun is being traversed to the rear. Both engine and transmission covers have louvres for the circulation of cooling air and a travelling clamp for the 120-mm. gun is hinged on the back of the exhaust silencer box. The Leopard hull is of simpler construction, being

built up from fabricated armour plate throughout although, again, the diameter of the turret ring necessitated a pannier design. The exhaust grilles are prominent features on both sides of these panniers.

Whereas the Chieftain driver sits centrally with stowage for ammunition and batteries on either side, the installation of the L7 gun in Leopard has resulted in the driver's position being shifted over to the right of the hull to ensure that the loader on the left of the gun has access to the large bin of ammunition alongside the driver. A unique and most successful feature in the Chieftain has been the reclining position for the driver when his hatch is closed and has permitted a significant reduction in the height of the hull. Access for both drivers is through a hatch of the "lift and swing" type and emergency exits can be made rearward into the fighting compartments. The Chieftain has a single wide-vision periscope behind the hatch and Leopard has three in front giving an arc of vision of some 130°. Both tanks have automated transmission systems although the Chieftain driver has direct control of the gear ratios which are

Above: *Leopard Main Battle Tank.*   (Krauss-Maffei)

Left: *Front view of Leopard.*

Bottom left: *Chieftain of the 17th/21st Lancers in Germany. The rubber pads inserted in the steel tracks limit damage to roads during training.*   (Army PR)

Below: *Chieftain Mark 2 of the 17th/21st Lancers. The layout of the fire control equipment and the excellent ballistic shape of the turret casting are noteworthy. The muzzles of the 0·5-in. ranging gun and the coaxial 7·62-mm. G.P. MG are visible to the right of and above the 120-mm. barrel respectively.*

(CCR)

Above: Standardpanzer *prototype with Type II turret mounting the 12·7-mm. ranging gun, later to be replaced by the cross-turret optical range finder.* (German MOD)

Right: *The driver's hatch in the centre of the glacis plate. The "lift and swing" hatch cover, the single, wide-view periscope behind the hatch itself and the non-slip surface on the armour are of interest in this Chieftain of the 1st Royal Tank Regiment.* (CCR)

selected by a foot pedal, not unlike that used on a motor cycle, while the selector lever in Leopard has only four positions: two forward ratios (road and cross country), reverse and neutral. Chieftain is steered by conventional levers and Leopard has a steering wheel. An interesting feature on Leopard is the provision of driving controls for the commander which, though limited in scope, enable him to retain a modicum of control if the driver is incapacitated or in similar emergencies.

The fighting compartment in both tanks extends the full width of the hull with the turrets suspended on ball races. The Chieftain turret is unconventional in design, the front being cast while the rear is fabricated from rolled armour plate. The high obliquity of its frontal and side aspects and the absence of a heavy mantlet are of particular interest (features which are shared with modern Soviet tanks) although the premium on internal stowage space and the need to balance the turret with its very long gun barrel have necessitated the addition of the rear bulge which contains gun control equipment, radios, ammunition and external stowage racks. The large light projector is mounted on the left side of the turret wall and will be returned to later in this section. The turret on Leopard is again of a much more simple construction and it has a rectangular mantlet on which the light projector is mounted; centrally on pre-production vehicles and offset to the left in later models. The shell is cast except for an oval roof plate which is welded into position. The positioning of the cross-turret range-finder forward of the gunner's position has necessitated a flattened top surface for the casting but it was considered that the disadvantages of a less than ideal ballistic shape were offset by the need to keep the overall height of the vehicle down and to free the commander from the minutiae of engaging targets. The bottom rear of the turret is chamfered to clear the raised roof of the power compartment. Both turrets have smoke grenade dischargers on the walls.

The turret crews occupy the same relative positions in both tanks, the loader on the left of the gun, the gunner opposite on the right with the commander

behind him. The radio equipment, however, is under the control of the commander in the Leopard (as it is in T-54) and of the loader in Chieftain. The L7A1 105-mm. armament in Leopard fires fixed rounds of three main natures—APDS, HESH and HEAT—the primers are initiated electrically and the empty cases are ejected into a canvas bag, this having spring-loaded covers. The recoil system consists of two hydraulic buffers and a pneumatic recuperator and is claimed to enhance the accuracy of the gun compared with the British layout in Centurion. A cradle on the left of the gun contains a 7·62-mm. MG1 and both this mounting, and the 105-mm. spent case bag, are connected to a fume-extracting system operated by a fan on the inside of the mantlet. The more powerful L11 120-mm. gun with its recoil system occupies a greater inboard volume in Chieftain than that of the L7 but this is offset by the use of separated ammunition (thus reducing the space needed to manoeuvre the rounds into the breech) and combustible bagged charges which do away with the need for a bin for spent cases as well as reducing the toxicity level in the turret atmosphere. But as obturation cannot be carried out by the walls of a shell case, as it is in the L7, a steel sleeve in the chamber and an insert on the face of the breech block are required for this function and the mechanism incorporates several fail-safe features. The breech block is of the falling wedge type and is opened automatically during run-out in a similar way to the L7. The charges are fired by vent tubes stored in a magazine on the breech ring and loaded automatically into the breech block where they are initiated electrically. The 120-mm. cradle is of the ring type and carries the recoil system consisting of two hydraulic buffers and a hydro-pneumatic recuperator, all three being secured to a yoke on the front of the breech ring. Two MGs are mounted on the left of the gun, the uppermost being in a cradle specially designed to ensure the stability of the 0·50-in. (12·7-mm.) ranging gun. This uses special tracer ammunition and the mechanism permits rapid series of three rounds each to be fired by the gunner operating a foot controller. The second more

Leopard demonstrating its agility in climbing a vertical step from the water. (Stern)

Chieftain manned by a crew from The Blues and Royals wading a shallow pool. (CCR)

White light from the Chieftain searchlight. (CCR)

Leopard moving at speed through a muddy lake. (Stern)

Camouflaged Leopard moving through woodland.

Chieftain with turret traversed, showing extent of rear bulge. (Army PR)

A dazzle-painted Chieftain of The Blues and Royals negotiating a knife-edged obstacle. (CCR)

Fourth Troop Leader of C Squadron The Blues and Royals supporting infantry as they leave their FV 432 APC. Note the resilient rubber rail round the engine compartment of the Chieftain to prevent damage when the 120-mm. gun is traversed rearwards, the access hatches on the rear roof of the turret and the large fuel fillers in the transmission decking.

(CCR)

Leopard driver's three periscopes in front give a 130° arc of vision. (German MOD)

Standardpanzer Prototype II during troop trials. (German MOD)

simple cradle contains the normal 7·62-mm. General Purpose MG (GPMG). Both main armament barrels have fume extractors and are usually fitted with thermal sleeves to minimize the possibility of bend, and consequent loss of accuracy, through the effects of differential heating or cooling. The design of the 105-mm. allows the barrel to be removed forwards very quickly but that on the 120-mm. has to be withdrawn through the rear of the turret. Experience having shown that most tank casualties are caused by ammunition fires, the opportunity has been taken in Chieftain to draw on naval experience and stow the 120-mm. charges in bins surrounded by pressurized water jackets.

Both tanks have conceptually similar facilities for laying the guns using power, hand and emergency modes, with over-riding controls for the commander.

However, while Chieftain has a development of the well-proven system used in Centurion incorporating a closed loop electro-servo stabilizing equipment in both elevation and azimuth axes, the Leopard has an electro-hydraulic Westinghouse equipment of the type used on the American M48 and M60 tanks. A Cadillac-Gage stabilizer may be fitted to Leopard as a later, retrospective modification.

The fire control systems are markedly different, that in Chieftain being a natural derivative from the one in Centurion. The commander in Chieftain is seated under a cupola which is made in two main assemblies. The static ring contains nine periscopes which give an uninterrupted, all-round view, and a reticle image projector connected to the gunner's sight mounting which defines the latter's alignment when the commander's sight is at the 12 o'clock

A production Leopard fitted with a thermal sleeve on the 105-mm. barrel. (German MOD)

A tank commander of The Blues and Royals wearing a respirator and protective clothing. He is observing through his binocular sight and grasping his controller for powered elevation and traverse with his right hand. (CCR)

A loader/operator of The Blues and Royals tuning one of the radio sets at the left rear of the turret. Two APDS projectiles are visible stowed on the turret sill with charge bins below the turret ring. (CCR)

Chieftain turret (above), driver's compartment (below).

1. Fixed fire extinguisher operating handles
2. Projectile locking handle
3. Rack lifting jack operating handle
4. Projectile rack
5. Fire alarm warning light
6. Reverse button
7. Lights switchbox
8. Driver's access door locking handle (left)
9. Driver's periscope mounting knurled nut
10. Generating unit engine switchbox
11. Driver's periscope swing bar
12. Driver's instrument panel
13. Driver's periscope
14. Driver's instrument panel mounting
15. Horn button
16. Main engine switch box
17. Periscope wiper parking lever
18. Periscope wiper motor
19. Radio distribution box
20. Driver's access door locking handle (right)
21. Driver's access door spring tube
22. Driver's safety switch
23. Fire extinguisher
24. Projectile locking handle
25. Rack retaining pin
26. Projectile rack
27. Battery thermal switch junction box
28. Bleed nipple
29. Main brake warning light pressure switch
30. Dozer equipment
31. Inspection light socket cover
32. Inter-vehicle starting socket cover
33. Driver's master switch
34. Steering lever lubricator
35. Right battery box
36. Right steering lever location pawl catch
37. Emergency gear lever locking plate
38. Generating unit engine governor control lever
39. Generating unit engine fuel cut-off lever
40. Emergency gear control lever
41. Right steering lever
42. Rack lifting jack
43. Accelerator pedal
44. Brake pedal
45. Driving lights dipswitch
46. Negative line junction box
47. Left steering lever
48. Gear selector pedal
49. Gear selector
50. Hydraulic starter pinion control lever
51. Hydraulic starter master cylinder reservoir
52. Hydraulic starter pump clutch lever
53. Left steering lever location pawl catch
54. Parking brake lever
55. Steering lever lubricator
56. Steering mechanism cross-shaft
57. Steering interlock lubricating nipple
58. Brake power valve
59. Release button (parking brake lever retaining pawl)
60. Fixed fire extinguishers
61. Left battery box

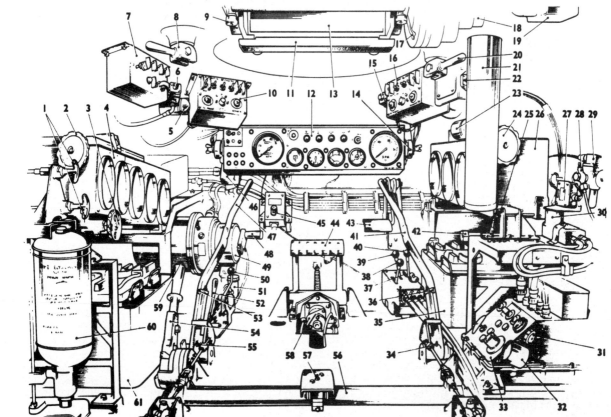

Chieftain at speed. (Army PR)

Production Leopard with combat carrier in front. (German MOD)

position. The rotating assembly contains the commander's binocular sight with a magnification of ten times ($\times 15$ on Mark 3), his 7·62-mm. MG which can be fired remotely from under armour, aimed by a graticule in the observation window of the sight, and a single hatch cover. The cupola can be rotated by means of a hand traversing gear to enable the commander to observe and acquire targets using his main sight, and by selecting "contrarotate" and gripping his duplex controller, the turret is driven into alignment with his line of sight. The gunner's equipment consists of a periscopic sight pivoting in the roof and connected to the gun cradle by a link bar whose length is maintained constant, despite changes in air temperature, by a compensating device. A ballistic graticule incorporates the range scales for APDS, HESH and the ranging gun (the latter having a pseudo-ballistic match with HESH up to about 1,300 metres in the Mark 2 and 2,500 metres in the Mark 3/3) and the 7·62-mm. MG. Ranging is accomplished by

firing series of the 0·50 in. rounds aimed by laying successive aiming dots on the target and observing which series either strikes or falls plus. The equivalent dot on the APDS scale is laid on the target and the 120-mm. gun fired: the first round in a HESH or smoke engagement is even more simple due to the common ballistic markings with the ranging gun. A range-drum and clinometer bubble are used for engagements beyond the range of the sight or when firing indirect, in conjunction with an electric traverse indicator. An alternative $\times 7$ sighting telescope is also available for direct fire only. The Mark 3/3 Chieftain will have an alternative ranging system in the Barr and Stroud LF2 laser instrument incorporated in the gunner's sight. With a 90 per cent chance of a system accuracy of plus or minus 10 metres to ranges well over 5,000 metres, engagements will become faster and more accurate. The 19-in., 2-3 kW light projector is used either for white light or near infra-red (IR) illumination and its aim is controlled automatically by

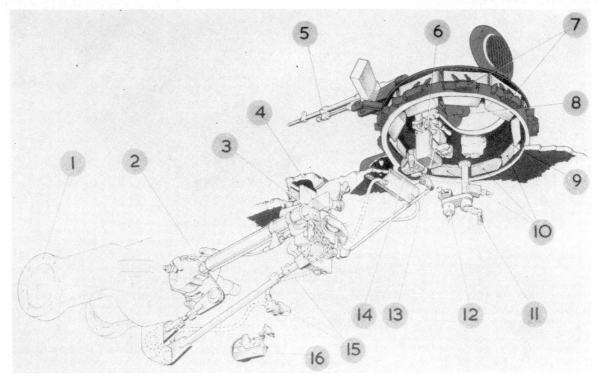

A general sketch of Chieftain fire control equipment. 1—Trunnion rings of 120-mm. cradle. 2—Gunner's telescopic sight. 3—Gunner's periscopic sight. 4—Hood with wiper equipment. 5—Commander's 7·62-mm. GPMG. 6—GPMG and sight elevating gear. 7—Periscope wipers. 8—IR spotlight. 9—Commander's rotatable cupola. 10—Periscopes (9). 11—Cupola traverse gear. 12—Cupola contra-rotation equipment. 13—Commander's periscopic binocular sight. 14—Collimator. 15—Temperature compensated link and pump. 16—Gunner's clinometer for semi- and fully indirect fire. (CCR)

a synchro system with the transmitter on the gunner's sight mounting. Both gunner's and commander's sights can be replaced by × 3 IR instruments whose optical systems contain image converter tubes to convert the reflected IR light into images visible to the human eye. The commander's spotlight can also be fitted with an IR filter and the system is completed by a detector which will give warning of IR illumination from any direction. The drivers on both tanks also have IR systems with a range of a few hundred metres. Passive Image intensification instruments are likely to replace IR in the future.

The commander of Leopard has a much simpler design of cupola, and a less comprehensive view through his seven fixed periscopes, although an intermediate position of the hatch cover allows him to observe over the top of the cupola sill. His main sight is a periscope mounted in the turret roof itself and the head can be rotated in azimuth independently of the turret. With its variable magnification of six to twenty times it is used for general observation, target acquisition and stadia ranging on targets of known dimensions. Once a target has been observed the commander can traverse the turret until the gunner's line of sight coincides with his own, the contra-rotation of the sight head and a flexible link to the azimuth indicator ensuring that the target will not be lost in the process. The tangent elevation of the gun

A hydraulically-operated dozer blade on a Chieftain Mark 1. (FVRDE, CCR)

A prototype Chieftain as it was first seen by the public. (CCR)

Close-up of Chieftain turret top with searchlight components removed.

Pre-production Leopards with Series III turrets.

is also transmitted electrically to the commander's periscope enabling him to lay and fire the guns in case of emergency. The gunner's sight is incorporated in the rangefinder which has a base length of 67 in. and a magnification of 16 times. Both stereoscopic and coincidence ranging can be selected the former being the more accurate and efficient in poor visibility while the latter is for the less skilful operators or those without stereoscopic vision. Movement of the wander marks and prisms in both the commander's and gunner's instruments is controlled by foot pedals. Tangent elevation appropriate to the nature of ammunition to be used is applied automatically to the gun as ranging proceeds. In principle, this layout bears a strong resemblance to that in the M47 tank although it has been improved upon considerably. An interesting feature is the shutter in the gunner's sight which closes for a quarter of a second when the 105-mm. is fired to prevent his being blinded by the flash. As in Chieftain, an alternative sighting telescope is provided and the commander's periscope can be replaced by an IR sight for viewing at night. An additional 7·62-mm. MG can be mounted to the forward edge of either the commander's or gunner's hatches but the firer has to expose himself to use it. Two periscopes are fitted in front of the loader's hatch on Leopard compared with one on Chieftain.

Both tanks have comprehensive heating and ventilation systems. The former in Leopard includes a fuel oil burning heater in the fighting compartment (again following American practice) that not only heats that compartment but can also be used to warm the engine coolant and the eight batteries to facilitate starting at low ambient temperatures. Air for ventilation in this tank is drawn in through a duct above the left track guard and filtered in a unit positioned in front of the large ammunition bin in the hull. The similar unit on Chieftain is mounted on the rear of the turret. Navigation systems can also be installed, that in Chieftain operating on the dead reckoning principle in which information from the speedometer drive and a gyro compass is analysed in a computer to derive position in the form of an eight figure grid reference and heading, both of which can be combined to plot the tank's movement on a map.

The engine in Leopard is the ten-cylinder, 37·4 litre, compression ignition, supercharged Daimler Benz DB 838 which can run on fuel oil or JP4 and delivers 830 b.h.p. at 2,200 r.p.m. It is a 90° upright Vee in layout and gives the tank an exceptional performance with an acceleration superior even to a number of light wheeled vehicles. At a sustained speed on roads of 40 m.p.h., a fuel consumption of about 1·7 m.p.g. and a capacity under armour of 220 imperial gallons Leopard has a radius of action of about 375 miles. Again, in keeping with American practice, the importance of a speedy removal and installation of the power plant and transmission is emphasized by the use of multiple connector plugs for electrical equipment, quick release couplings for fuel and other hydraulic pipes and all mechanical linkages have quick release pins and clips. A 9 kW 3-phase alternator

Leopard with schnorkel tower in place advancing through smoke to river crossing. (German MOD)

Chieftain emerging from a deep-wading pit. The commander is standing at the top of the schnorkel tower. (Keystone)

Pre-production Standardpanzer, with the bottom section of the schnorkel tower only fitted, reversing at speed from a wading tank. (German MOD)

Leopard Standardpanzer crossing the River Rhine at Koln-Westhoven in July 1964. (Deutsche Press-Agentur)

An early Leopard undergoing deep-wading tests which include stopping and re-starting the engine while submerged.

Leopard with a gunfire simulator mounted on the 105-mm. barrel. (GermanMOD)

is driven from the engine and a silicon rectifier is used to convert the output to DC. This arrangement permits the batteries to be charged even when the engine is idling quietly and obviates the need for an auxiliary engine. The Chieftain two-stroke L60 main engine has six vertical cylinders with opposed pistons, a capacity of 19 litres and produces 650 b.h.p. (730 gross SAE) at 2,100 r.p.m. running on fuel oil. The maximum road speed governed at 25 m.p.h. and a range of about 250 miles are markedly less than those for Leopard*, reflecting the differing priorities for mobility, although acceleration from a standing start and the sustained speeds of both across country are not significantly different. A Coventry Climax A30, with three cylinders and six vertically opposed pistons drives a 24-volt 350-amp dc generator to supplement a 150-amp machine powered by the L60.

Drive from the L60 is transmitted through a centrifugal clutch, which becomes operative at a crankshaft speed of about 320 r.p.m., to the TN12 gearbox which is a combined change speed and steering unit using a Wilson epicyclic gear train and a Merritt differential steering system. The six forward and three reverse gears are engaged by brake bands applied hydraulically. A governor is incorporated to prevent changes up at low engine speeds and initiates changes down when the engine speed drops below 800 r.p.m. The main and steering brakes are of the disc type, also operated hydraulically, and drive to the sprocket is

through a single 5:1 reduction gear. The transmission on Leopard consists of a single stage torque converter and the top three gear ratios have a "lock-up" facility to reduce power losses, and thereby fuel consumption, on road moves. Changes of ratio are made electro-hydraulically, although second gear can be engaged mechanically in case of a power failure. The steering mechanism is also integral with the gearbox and is of the two radii, regenerative type. This gives an infinitely variable range for the wider turns and fixed, gear-related radii for tight turns: a complete neutral turn on concrete can be made in ten seconds.

The suspension on Leopard consists of transversely mounted torsion bars with seven road wheel stations on either side—the first three and the last two incorporating hydraulic shock absorbers. The double pin type tracks with rubber pads are American in design and they can be replaced by anti-skid combat tracks. The top rollers are unusual in that two support the inside, and the other two the outside, of the track. Chieftain continues to use the modified Horstmann design that proved successful on Centurion and Conqueror, the three units on both sides having two road wheels each mounted on axle arms bearing against a pack of horizontal springs. The front units only have shock absorbers. The track plates are made of cast manganese steel with removable rubber pads; they are connected by dry pins and stretch is compensated for by moving the adjuster wheel forward on its eccentric mounting. Again, in common with Centurion, the side armour of the hull is given additional protection by the use of detachable spring-steel plates.

Both tanks are capable of deep wading, the Chieftain to a depth of 15 ft. and Leopard to 16·5 ft., using a wide tower over the commander's hatch for the air supply, commander's control position and as an emergency escape route.

---

* The figures for the Chieftain Mark 3 have been raised to 30 m.p.h. and 310 miles respectively. The Mark 5 will have an L60 developing 750 b.h.p.; 840 gross at the SAE rating.

Top left: A Chieftain power pack removed. Note the radiator shown in the raised position and the two fans under the hydraulic cooler reservoir. (Army PR)

Bottom left: The power pack being lifted out of a Chieftain. (Army PR)

Below: A Chieftain clutch and gearbox assembly, the power pack having been removed from the hull. (Army PR)

Lifting the power pack and transmission of a Leopard for servicing.
(Soldat und Technik)

An anti-aircraft version of Leopard designed by Oerlikon-Contraves, mounting two 35-mm. guns under radar control.
(Oerlikon)

FV 4025 bridgelayer on Chieftain chassis with the folding spans in the travelling position.
(FVRDE, CCR)

Bergepanzer armoured recovery vehicle lifting a complete Leopard power unit, with a second unit on the rear platform.
(Atlas-Mak)

A small-scale model of a design for a bridgelayer based on a Leopard chassis.
(Soldat und Technik)

Bridgelayer Leopard Type A.   (Krauss-Maffei)

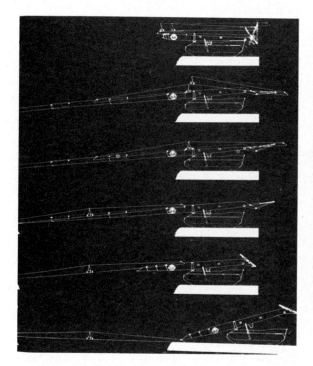

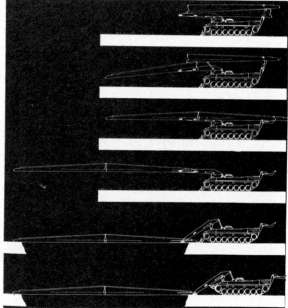

Above: *Diagram showing bridge in position. (Type B).*

Left: *Diagram showing bridge in position. (Type A).*

Bridgelayer Leopard Type B.   (Krauss-Maffei)

Another Leopard variant is the armoured engineer vehicle. (Krauss-Maffei)

CONCLUSION

These two tanks have been designed to defeat a common enemy on the same type of terrain and in the context of the same alliance; and yet their basic characteristics differ widely. Part of the explanation may be sought in the experiences of World War 2 where, on the British side, poorly armed and armoured tanks defeated their opponents primarily through superior numbers and mobility. Yet casualties were high and there seems little doubt that those deficiencies have influenced British design ever since the inception of Centurion in 1943. The expected disparity in numbers in a future European war has tended to reinforce the insistence on a powerful combination of weapons and protection. The Germans, for their part, saw the weight of their tanks rise ten times in as many years, but their chance of survival

on the battlefield against the proliferation of anti-tank weapons down to infantry section level decreased considerably. In addition, the need to build special bridges and transport in order to maintain some semblance of mobility on the battlefield convinced the Germans that the vicious spiral upwards of weight must be cut short. Although armour could not be discarded entirely, speed and shock action of armour manoeuvring *en masse* would more than make up for the reduction in passive protection, and these principles were added special point when considering operations on a nuclear battlefield where swift concentrations of effort from initial dispersal would be vital.

These arguments can be countered if it is accepted that there is a finite limit to the speed at which a tank with the present, conventional types of sus-

Leopard adapted for tank driving school. (Krauss-Maffei)

pension can cross broken ground without the turret crew being little more than hapless passengers longing for the journey to end. If this is the case then the efficiency of the tank as a weapon system during such moves is almost nullified. Added to this, it is difficult to see that the raising of the top speed in these conditions alters significantly the chance of hit by automated missiles flying at near-supersonic velocities, or modern guns with advanced fire control systems. In other words, it would be more economical to limit damage when once hit than to try to avoid hit at all. Again, on examining the history of armoured warfare there is little or no evidence to suggest that the lack of speed alone in tanks has ever been a decisive cause for failure in any operation. Where failures occurred they were more likely to have been precipitated by shortcomings in command, training and logistics, to mention but a few. If a significant increase in the tempo of operations is sought it seems more logical to concentrate on these—admittedly

more intractable—factors, than on the addition of a few miles an hour to the top speed.

A further doctrinal difference involves the tactical handling of armour. Whereas the British view is that the best killer of a tank is another tank, and this process must start at long range, the Germans have long held that specialized anti-tank weapons are a better answer to attacks by armour and they use either the 25-ton Jpz 4-5 self-propelled gun mounting a 90-mm. gun or a similar chassis carrying SS 11 missiles for this purpose alone.

There is little doubt that these differences in opinion will dissolve in time when the increasing efficiency of power plants and new designs of suspension will permit the tank of the future to be better armed, armoured and more agile. But for the present the highly efficient gun and armour combination that is Chieftain and the less sophisticated but superbly mobile tank that is Leopard, will remain as tantalizing alternatives on the mechanized battlefield.

Leopards on manoeuvres. (German MOD)

Side view of Leopard with tactical markings on turret. (German MOD)

Though slower on the road than Leopard, Chieftain Mark 2's sustained cross country speed is not significantly different.
(Army PR)

Head-on view of Leopard. (Krauss-Maffei)

Above: *The power pack of Chieftain being lifted out by REME fitters. The two cooling fans can be seen with, immediately above, the radiators that have been raised to the vertical position.*
(FVRDE, CCR)

A general head-on view of a Chieftain Mark 2 of the 1st Royal Tank Regiment as it moves closed-down. (CCR)

Later Developments

(by Duncan Crow)

Chieftain, like Centurion before it, is now on its way through a continuing life of improvements. Marks 1, 2, 3 and 5 are described in Lieutenant-Colonel Norman's Profile of the tank. Mark 3/3 has a laser sight. Mark 4 was a design study only. Mark 5 with new fire control becomes Mark 8. Mark 6 is Mark 2 brought up to Mark 5 standard and with new fire control becomes Mark 9. Mark 7 is Mark 3/3 brought up to Mark 5 standard and with new fire control becomes Mark 10.

Mark 5P is the version which has been sold to Iran. It was announced in June 1976 that the next order of Chieftains to be built for Iran would include the new Chobham armour which gives considerably more protection for a given weight, as well as a new 1,200 bhp Rolls-Royce engine, a redesigned hull and turret, a new David Brown transmission, and the latest fire control equipment.

Leading characteristics of Chieftain Mark 5 are:

Engine, make	L 60No.4Mk7A
horse power	710
Fuel capacity	950 litres
Range, roads	500 km
Weight, unloaded	52,800 kg
combat loaded	54,800 kg
Power to weight ratio	15.5 HP/t
Ground pressure	0.84 kg/cm²
Length with gun forward	10.80 m
with gun in travelling lock	7.51 m
Width without skirts	3.33 m
with skirts	3.50 m
with IR searchlight	3.66 m
Height overall	2.87 m
Ground clearance	0.52 m
Maximum road speed	44 km/hr
Gun, calibre	120mm
length	55 calibres
ammunition carried	54 rounds
Secondary armament, coaxial	7.62mm MG L8A1
machine-gun, external	7.62mm L37A1
machine-gun, ranging, coaxial	12.7mm L21A1
Crew	4

As well as the Chieftain gun tank, to which a dozer blade can be added that is operated hydraulically, there is a Chieftain bridgelayer with a folding "scissors" span of 75ft and a Chieftain armoured recovery vehicle.

Leopard, too, is proceeding through a development sequence. After the Standardpanzer came Leopard 1 which has appeared in four Ausfuehrungen: A1, A2, A3 and A4. A1 has a stabiliser, scalloped skirts, thermal jacket, bow vane, tracks with replacement pads, and deep wading kit. A2 is the same with a cast turret, hull louvers without vertical bars, improved CBR protection, and night vision equipment. A3 has an automatic loader and a welded spaced armour turret. A4 is the same with new fire control equipment.

Following Leopard 1 has come Leopard 2 which is not just a re-design of Leopard 1 but is a development of the Kampfpanzer 70 (Keiler, wild boar), the German designation for the joint F.R.G.-U.S. tank project called in America the MBT 70. In 1970 each country decided to go its own way on the design, but in neither did the tank go into production although a number of prototypes were built. Leopard 2 has the Leopard A3 turret design, a 120mm automatic smoothbore gun using fin-stabilised ammunition, laser range-finder, stabiliser, and MBT 70 power train.

A word may be said in passing about the MBT 70. Although it looked like a conventional battle tank it departed from traditional practice by having all three members of the crew in the turret. The driver was provided with a counter-rotating turret so that he was always facing the direction of the tank's movement regardless of the way the turret was turned. The need for a fourth crew member was avoided by the use of an automatic loader. The tank also had an adjustable hydro-pneumatic suspension. Its most controversial feature was its main armament, the 152mm gun/launcher.

The MBT 70 was simplified to produce the cheaper XM 803. But even in this austere form it did not go into production and by 1975 when, as Colonel Icks says in his Profile of the M48-M60 series, the MBT 70/XM 803 was expected to be ready for service, the whole project had been abandoned at the behest of the U.S. Congress because of its cost.

Subsequently the U.S. proceeded to the design of the XM1 MBT and the Germans to a joint Anglo-German project the MBT 80 or Leopard 3, one prototype of which is turretless like the Swedish Strv 103.

Leading characteristics of the Leopard A2 and A3 are:

Engine, make	MTU MB 838 Ca D500
horse power	830
Fuel capacity	985 litres
Range, roads	600 km
Weight, unloaded	40,400 kg
combat loaded	42,400 kg
Power to weight ratio	19.7 HP/t
Ground pressure	0.90 km/cm²
Length with gun forward	9.54 m
with gun in travelling lock	8.17 m
Width without skirts	3.25 m
with skirts	3.37 m
Height overall	2.62 m
Ground clearance	0.44 m
Maximum road speed (forward)	65 km/hr
(in reverse)	25 km/hr
Gun, calibre	105mm
length	51 calibres
ammunition carried	60 rounds
Secondary armament	two 7.62mm MG3
Crew	4

As well as the gun tank the Leopard "family" consists of a Bergepanzer (Armoured Recovery Vehicle), Pionierpanzer (Armoured Engineer Vehicle), Brückenlegerpanzer (Bridgelayer), and Flakpanzer (Anti-aircraft Tank). The Leopard chassis is also used for the SP70 self-propelled 155mm howitzer.

Original production version of Strv 103, or S-tank type A, without flotation gear.

S — Tank

Tank design has tended to follow a well-established pattern. In consequence, battle tanks resemble each other to a large extent. But there are exceptions to this, the most notable being the controversial Swedish S-tank which differs in many important respects from all other tanks.

The most obvious feature of the S-tank is its lack of a turret. This alone makes it unconventional but does not, in itself, represent anything new. In fact, the very first tanks were turretless and so have been many others. What makes the S-tank different and an advance on all the earlier turretless vehicles is that the mounting of its gun is fixed in relation to the hull. As a result, it possesses several important advantages over other, more conventional, turreted as well as turretless vehicles.

Because it has no turret, the S-tank is considerably lower than conventional, turreted tanks, which makes it a more difficult target to hit. Moreover, its fixed gun mounting has eliminated the need for the space required within the armour envelope of turreted and even more of turretless vehicles by the movement of the breech end of the gun. The fixed gun mounting has also made it possible to install a relatively simple automatic loading mechanism, since it eliminates angular movement between the gun and the ammunition magazine. This, in turn, made it possible to dispense with the human loader and thus save a considerable amount of space within the vehicle, making the S-tank even more compact and consequently also lighter.

These and other advantages of the S-tank imply, however, that its gun can only be elevated or depressed by altering the pitch of the hull and traversed only by turning the whole vehicle. In other words, its gun can only be aimed by moving the whole vehicle. This had not been done before and it was only after several years of development that this method was successfully established.

ORIGINS OF THE DESIGN

Ideas which led to the S-tank originated with Sven Berge, the head of the tank design section of the Vehicle Division of the Swedish Army Ordnance. They arose out of his studies of tanks which had been produced by the early fifties and especially of the French AMX–13. At the time the Swedish Army actually considered purchasing this light tank from France although in the end it bought the more powerful Centurions from Britain. Nevertheless, some features of the AMX–13 attracted Berge, as they did other tank designers. In particular, he recognised the advantages of AMX–13's novel oscillating or trunnion-mounted turret. This allowed the gun to be mounted closer than ever to the turret roof, so that the tank needed to expose itself less when firing, and simplified fire control equipment and the installation of an automatic loading mechanism, because the gun did not move in relation to the optical instruments and the ammunition magazine. All these advantages accrued from the fact that the gun of the AMX–13 was fixed in the upper part of its two-piece oscillating turret and was elevated or depressed with it. However, the oscillating turret also had its disadvantages

Lvkv 42, an experimental 40-mm. self-propelled anti-aircraft gun with an adjustable suspension built by Bofors in 1954.

and this led Berge to propose an alternative way of exploiting its good features in the form of a turretless vehicle with a fixed gun mounting.

The origin of the ideas which led to the S-tank is particularly interesting because in retrospect it appears as a logical development of the earlier assault guns and other turretless vehicles. In fact, historically and from other points of view it is at least as much a development of turreted tanks, with the turret mounted directly on a tracked suspension.

PRELIMINARY INVESTIGATIONS

Berge put forward his original proposal in August 1956. At the time some of the concepts embodied in it had already been partly proved and this had, in fact, contributed to the formulation of the proposal. In particular, AB Bofors, the Swedish company world-famous for its guns, developed between 1949 and 1954 an experimental self-propelled 40-mm. anti-aircraft gun with an adjustable hydro-mechanical suspension which showed the feasibility of elevating or depressing a gun by altering the pitch of the hull in which it was mounted. The feasibility of traversing the gun by turning a vehicle was less clear. That the gun could be swung rapidly using a vehicle's clutch-and-brake steering system was shown several years earlier when the Swedish Army tested a German assault gun, the *Sturmgeschütz III,* as well as several other foreign vehicles acquired for evaluation purposes after the Second World War. But whether the gun could also be traversed sufficiently smoothly and accurately remained to be proved: the *Sturmgeschütz* and all but one other vehicle with hull-mounted guns could move them to a limited extent in relation to the hull for fine traverse.

The one exception was the French *Char B* of the thirties. This battle tank had a hull-mounted 75-mm. gun which was elevated independently of the hull but which was traversed by turning the vehicle by means of a double-differential steering mechanism with a hydro-static steering drive. The steering system was derived

from the SRB experimental tank designed in 1921 under the direction of E. Brillié, of the Schneider company, who had designed the first French tank. It provided a positive, infinitely variable degree of control over the speed of the tracks which made it superior for many years to other steering systems. However, in spite of the excellent steering system, the method of aiming the 75-mm. gun of the *Char B* by turning the whole tank did not prove entirely satisfactory after the tank was put into service in 1936 and was eventually abandoned. Thus on the final *Char B1 ter* version, of which only five were built before the French Army was defeated in 1940, the gun was no longer fixed in traverse but could be moved, independently of the hull, over an arc of 10 degrees.

The experience of the French Army with the *Char B* did not discourage Berge nor did it prevent his proposal from being accepted for further study by the Swedish Army Ordnance. However, it clearly indicated the need to reexamine the problem of gun laying by turning a vehicle very carefully. This was first explored in the winter of 1957–58 at the Swedish Armoured Centre at Skövde using an IKV 103, a light turretless 105-mm. assault gun built by AB Landsverk and Bofors, fitted with a "crowbar" steering system.

In essence, the "crowbar" system consisted of a lever on either side of the vehicle, one end of each lever being pivoted on the hull and the other having a foot which could be made to rest on the track and move it when the lever was rotated about the pivot by a hydraulic ram mounted on a frame attached to the front of the vehicle. The "crowbar" system fitted to the IKV 103 provided a simple method of precise control over small track movement and proved that a gun could be aimed with sufficient accuracy by turning a vehicle with an appropriate steering system.

The results obtained with the IKV 103 were verified in 1959 using the chassis of a U.S. M4 Sherman medium tank. In this case the levers of the "crowbar" system were located between the tracks and the hull and the

IKV 103 assault gun with an experimental, external "crowbar" steering system.

hydraulic rams were inside the hull superstructure, over the tracks, which made it all look much tidier. However, the main reason for building the second test rig was to check that there were no unforeseen scale effects between the 9-ton IKV 103 and the proposed tank which like the Sherman chassis was expected to weigh about 30 tons. The Sherman chassis was also fitted with a 150-mm. gun without recoil gear to explore the effects of rigidly mounting guns, which was originally proposed in Germany towards the end of the Second World War. The rigid mounting proved acceptable but it was not pursued further.

COMPONENT DEVELOPMENT

In the meantime, on the strength of the results obtained with the IKV 103 and paper studies, Bofors were awarded a contract in mid-1958 to develop the proposed turretless tank with a fixed gun mounting. This was to embody such novel features as an adjustable hydropneumatic suspension, a new steering system and an automatic loading mechanism.

Bofors had by then only designed two armoured vehicles and neither got beyond the prototype stage. One was the Lvkv 42, the 13.5-ton 40-mm. self-propelled anti-aircraft gun with an adjustable suspension built for the Swedish Army in 1954; the other was a 20-ton turretless 120-mm. assault gun with an automatic loading mechanism which was built by Bofors on their own initiative in the late forties. However, both vehicles incorporated original features which foreshadowed those of the S-tank and Bofors were well qualified to undertake its development not only because of this but even more because of their very considerable experience of naval and anti-aircraft gun control systems which was

Sherman medium tank chassis with an internal "crowbar" steering system.

Bofors 120-mm. experimental assault gun with automatic loading.

highly relevant to a sophisticated fighting vehicle such as the S-tank.

Moreover, Bofors were assisted in the development of the S-tank by AB Volvo, Sweden's leading motor manufacturers, who were brought into it in 1959 as subcontractors for the power plant, and by AB Landsverk, who became subcontractors for much of the running gear. A little earlier, in May 1959, Bofors received an order from the Swedish Army for the construction of two prototypes.

At about the same time the Swedish Army also decided to abandon the development of an earlier, turreted battle tank, the Strv KRV, designed by AB Landsverk who had been Sweden's leading tank producers since 1930. This was a 45-ton vehicle powered by a specially developed 850 h.p. V–12 air-cooled spark ignition engine which was to have been fitted with a large Bofors-designed turret mounting a smooth-bore automatically-loaded 150-mm. gun. However the turret was never made and the two KRV tank chassis which had been built by 1957 were converted into test rigs for the S-tank components. In the process the number of road wheels was reduced from six per side to four so that in this respect, as well as in their 30-ton weight, they would resemble the S-tank. The modified chassis were then fitted with the hydro-pneumatic suspension intended for the S-tank, which was extensively tested in them during 1960, and a new steering mechanism with a hydrostatic steering drive. Finally one of them was also fitted with a high-velocity gun—the 83.4-mm. 20-pounder of the contemporary Centurions. Thus, even before the first prototype of the S-tank was completed, its basic components had been extensively tested and its general characteristics were being proved.

Small-scale model of the 45-ton KRV battle tank which was to have been fitted with an automatically-loaded smooth-bore 150-mm. gun.

SUSPENSION AND STEERING

The final proof of the S-tank concept was provided by the two prototypes which were completed in 1961 and which for the first time incorporated all its essential features. The hydro-pneumatic suspension which allowed the pitch of the hull to be changed includes four road wheels per side, the front and third wheels being mounted on leading arms and the second and fourth on trailing arms. Each arm is connected to a piston in a hydraulic cylinder and this, in turn, is hydraulically connected to a second, or spring, cylinder where a floating piston separates the hydraulic fluid from the springing medium, which is nitrogen. The cylinder assemblies of the two centre wheels on each side are independent of each other and the rest of the system. But the front and rear wheel suspension units are connected diagonally across the vehicle, e.g. the front right unit is connected to the rear left unit, and each hydraulic interconnection includes a positive displacement pump which can transfer fluid from the front to the rear unit, or vice versa. This changes the pitch of the hull by altering the setting of the road wheel arms and consequently elevates the gun to a maximum of 12 degrees above the horizontal or depresses it 10 degrees below the horizontal.

Changes in the attitude of the hull inevitably involve changes in the length of the track which had to be compensated for. The usual method by mechanical

control of the idler position was deemed too cumbersome and so another electro-hydraulic servo system was added to the two diagonally interconnected suspension systems. This alters the height of the hull above the ground by simultaneously adding or subtracting an equal amount of fluid from the front and rear units and thereby compensates for changes in track length.

Between each pair of cylinders there is a special valve to damp vehicle motion and there is also a hydraulic interconnection between the four front and rear units which provides the equivalent of a stable, three-point support for the hull. In addition there are cut-off valves which can isolate any of the four units should it get damaged while hull pitch control is still possible with the other three units. To make it rugged the suspension system has been made to operate at a relatively low pressure, even though this has made it somewhat less compact. The most vulnerable parts of the suspension, namely the road wheels, are the same as those of the Centurions so that they can be replaced more easily from a common stock of spares.

The second of the two major problems associated with a fixed gun mounting has been solved by a novel two-stage steering system. In essence, it consists of a double-differential mechanism with a hydrostatic steering drive and a superimposed clutch-and-brake system which comes into operation when sharp turns are

Prototype of the KRV battle tank with a cylindrical weight simulating its turret.

Chassis of the KRV modified into a test rig for the S-tank's hydropneumatic suspension and steering system.

Test rig based on the KRV chassis fitted with a 83.4-mm. 20-pounder of the Centurion.

required. Thus, the steering system of the S-tank operates in two stages. In the first instance it behaves as a double-differential system, so that it is regenerative and there is no loss of vehicle speed during steering movements. At the same time the hydrostatic steering drive makes the steering infinitely variable and provides the smooth traverse control necessary for laying the gun accurately on target. In the second stage of steering, when one of the clutches is disengaged and the associated brake is applied, the steering behaves like a geared system with a large step-down. This enables the S-tank to change direction very rapidly—so much so that it can swing its gun round as quickly, or quicker, than the turret of a conventional tank.

The provision of hull pitch control and of a two-stage steering system has not, for all its inevitable complexity, brought in any complication from the vehicle users' point of view. The S-tank is, in fact, simpler to operate than other tanks due to the integration of the steering and gun controls into a single unit which consists of a box with handle-bars. Rotation of the box about a vertical axis steers the vehicle: the first 23 degrees of rotation control the hydrostatic steering unit while further rotation actuates the clutch-and-brake system. Twisting the handle-bars, on the other hand, alters the pitch of the hull. In addition the control box contains a number of push buttons for loading and firing the main and auxiliary armament.

Both the driver and the commander of the S-tank are provided with such a control unit and each also has an accelerator and a brake pedal, so that either can operate the tank by himself, the commander being able to override the gunner. Normally the driver is also expected to act as the gunner but if a target is to be engaged quickly the commander, who is likely to acquire it first, can do it by himself. Thus the commander does not have to go through the usual motions of issuing orders to other crew members who then have to react to them before a target can be engaged.

The driver/gunner and the commander are located

Unit of the Bofors hydro-pneumatic suspension.

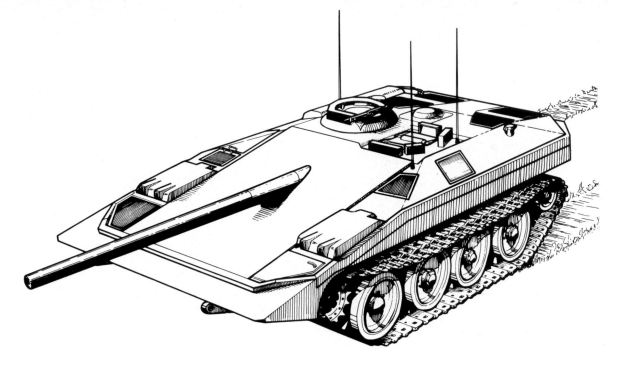

Drawing of the S-tank prototype which shows the original pair of machine-gun boxes with two 7.62-mm. machine-guns in each.

Steering and suspension control unit with loading and firing buttons for the main and auxiliary armament.

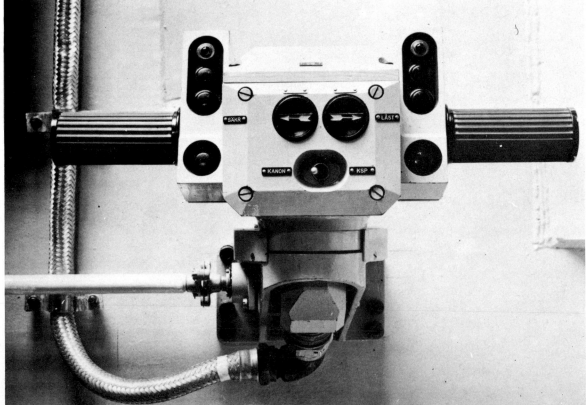

S-tank prototype with the original all-steel track.

Sectioned drawing of the S-tank in prototype form which shows the forward location of the engines and transmission and the rear location of the ammunition magazine.

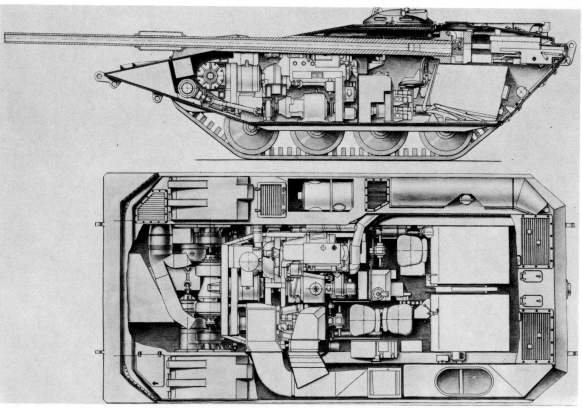

Side view of S-tank pre-production model without machine-gun boxes.

abreast of each other in the centre of the tank. Behind the driver and facing rearwards is the third member of the S-tank's three-man crew—a radio operator who is also provided with a simplified set of driving controls so that he can drive the tank backwards. Its ability to be driven backwards as easily as forwards is peculiar to the S-tank and gives it a unique advantage in this respect over others. The rearward facing location of the third crewman also means that he can keep a constant watch over the rear sector of the S-tank which gives it another unique advantage over other tanks.

ARMAMENT SYSTEM

Between the driver/gunner and the commander is the S-tank's 105-mm. gun. The gun is very similar to the British L7 105-mm. gun used in several tanks, including the final versions of the Centurion, the U.S. M60, the German Leopard, the Swiss Pz.61 and the Anglo-Indian Vickers Vijayanta, and it can fire the same type of ammunition. This is particularly important to the Swedish Army as it has a considerable number of Centurions in its armoured units. However, the gun is made in Sweden by Bofors and is 62 instead of 51 calibres long, which gives its APDS projectiles a muzzle velocity significantly higher than the 1450 m/sec of the shorter barrelled gun. The higher muzzle velocity gives, in turn, greater penetration, the resulting improvement being equivalent to penetrating a typical armour plate at 500 metres longer range. At the same time the sector swept by the gun when traversed is smaller than that swept by shorter turret-mounted guns because its breech is located towards the rear of the tank.

Behind the crew compartment, at the rear of the hull, is a 50 round ammunition magazine for the gun with a hydraulically-operated automatic loading mechanism.

The magazine is split into two halves on the centre line of the vehicle, one half normally containing APDS and the other HE rounds. The rounds are stowed in ten racks and descend by gravity on to a loading tray from where they are transported to the centre of the magazine area by a hydraulic ram—one to each magazine half. Once a round reaches the centre of the floor another ram lifts it to the level of the breech and a fourth pushes it home. After the round has been fired the empty case is automatically ejected through a trap door in the rear hull plate. Since there is no relative movement between the gun mounting and the ammunition magazine the whole installation is relatively simple and trouble free. The magazine is reloaded from outside through two hatches in the rear hull plate and two men can do it in approximately 10 minutes, which is considerably less than the time required to stow more conventional turreted tanks as well as being less fatiguing.

Apart from eliminating the need for a human loader, saving space and making all rounds immediately available for firing, the automatic loader of the S-tank has also increased the rate of fire to 15 rounds per minute, which is almost twice the rate of fire of tanks with manually loaded rounds of the same calibre. Its rate of fire is such in fact that the S-tank could fire its 105-mm. gun in bursts, to increase the probability of destroying a particularly dangerous target, and the possibility of doing this is increased by the automatic lock-out of the suspension whenever the gun firing button is pressed, which makes it practicable to fire successive rounds without relaying.

In addition to its main armament, the S-tank in the prototype form was to be fitted with four 7.62-mm. machine-guns mounted in pairs in armoured boxes on each side of the frontal hull plate. All four were to be sighted in parallel with the 105-mm. gun and fired by

87

remote control. The commander's rotating cupola was similar to that fitted at about the same time to the Pbv 301 armoured personnel carrier and like the latter was to have been fitted with an externally mounted 20mm. automatic gun. However, the mounting of the latter was considered too vulnerable for the S-tank and it was never fitted.

ENGINE INSTALLATION

As the rear of the hull was taken up by the ammunition magazine the engine and transmission compartment had to be located at the front. It contains, in fact, two different engines mounted alongside each other and geared to a common output, one engine being a diesel and the other a gas turbine.

When it was adopted for the S-tank the combination of a diesel with a gas turbine had only been tried in warships. There it offered the advantage of the economy of the diesel for cruising and of being able to provide the additional power required for limited periods of time from the relatively compact gas turbine. Similar considerations led to the adoption of the combination for the S-tank. Thus the diesel was intended to be used alone under normal running conditions, when the power demand of tanks is low, and the gas turbine was to be switched on only for the relatively infrequent periods when a large amount of power is needed. Such an arrangement not only exploited the efficiency of the

diesel and the high specific output of the gas turbine but also minimised the inefficiency of the latter by confining its operation to peak power periods.

The use of the gas turbine also offered the advantage of it being easily started, particularly under cold weather conditions, and it could be used as a starter engine for the diesel when the temperature was very low—an important point under Sweden's winter conditions. The gear train coupling the two engines also allowed either to be used by itself to drive the tank in an emergency, which halved the common risk of the tank being immobilised by an engine failure.

The diesel which was actually chosen was the Rolls-Royce K-60, a 6-cylinder opposed-piston water-cooled two-stroke which had just been developed to a British Army requirement. However, the two S-tank prototypes still had to be fitted with its spark-ignition predecessor, the 8-cylinder Rolls-Royce B.81 which developed 230 b.h.p. When it became available the K-60 provided 240 b.h.p. and was coupled to a Volvo hydro-kinetic torque converter automatic transmission whose output is combined with that from the gas turbine to drive the tracks. The K-60 also drives the hydrostatic steering unit through a power take-off.

The gas turbine was the American-made Boeing 502-10MA, a simple unit without a heat exchanger and consequently relatively inefficient, but compact and proved, having been used in quantity by the U.S. Navy. It developed 330 b.h.p. but provided more power than a

Left, Rolls-Royce K.60 diesel and, right, Boeing 502–10MA gas turbine with the gear train which couples them to the output shafts.

S-tank, left, compared with a conventional, turreted Centurion tank.

S-tank pre-production model with the original, domed commander's cupola.

Rear view of an S-tank pre-production model which shows the location of the radiator louvres.

Pre-production models of the S-tank during trials: note the absence of the machine-gun boxes.

Pre-production version of the S-tank with a 12.7-mm. ranging machine-gun in the right hand machine-gun box.

piston engine of the same nominal output because it did not have to drive cooling fans which consume a significant fraction of the gross horse power of piston engines.

The Boeing gas turbine was to have been replaced in time by a more efficient Volvo gas turbine with a heat exchanger but the latter did not materialize. Eventually another, more powerful Boeing model succeeded the original one and more than made up for the power which was earlier expected to come from further development of the K-60 diesel. At different times various other high output diesels were also considered, as they became available, as a possible replacement by themselves for the diesel-gas turbine combination, but none was able to provide as much power and fit in the available space.

PROBABILITY OF SURVIVAL

The location of the engine compartment at the front of the S-tank complicated access to it. In fact, provision had to be made for removing the front glacis plate which was split into three parts. Thus, a part of the frontal armour on either side of the central portion can be unbolted and swung over the centre to provide sufficient access for maintenance of the engine under it. But to replace the diesel the central portion of the plate and the gun barrel also have to be removed.

On the other hand, the location of the engines in front of the crew compartment has increased the protection against attack from the most probable direction. The main protection over the frontal arc is, of course, provided by the glacis plate which is exceptionally well sloped due to the S-tank's peculiar configuration and is therefore particularly effective against high-velocity armour-piercing projectiles. Its effectiveness has been further increased by the addition of a series of horizontal ribs, or rectangular bars, which deflect armour-piercing projectiles and thereby increase protection for less weight than the addition of conventional, solid armour plate. Ribbed armour was not, however, used on either of the prototypes as this would have revealed it prematurely.

Additional protection has also been gained against attack by shaped charge projectiles or rockets by placing the main fuel tanks outside the hull above the tracks. The vulnerability of the S-tank is also reduced by the relatively low location of its gun ammunition, which is the most serious source of fires in tanks whose armour has been perforated.

The S-tank's chances of survival on a battlefield are also greatly increased by its low silhouette. Its height, measured to the top of the roof, is in fact only 1.9 metres compared with a height of at least 2.3 or 2.4 metres for turreted tanks. In consequence it presents a much more difficult target to enemy weapons and its probability of being hit is considerably reduced. For instance, when fired at in the open at 1000 metres by a typical tank gun with no sophisticated fire control equipment its probability of being hit is 12 per cent lower than that of the lowest of contemporary turreted battle tanks. Its chances of avoiding being hit are even greater than this figure would indicate because the bottom metre, or so, of any tank is usually hidden by the unevenness of the ground, which means that the percentage difference between the exposed heights of the S-tank and of a turreted tank is considerably greater than the difference between their actual heights. Thus when the bottom metre of both types is ignored the chances of a hit at 1000 metres become 34 per cent lower for the S-tank. To put it in yet another way, the probability of the S-tank being hit is only about 60 per cent that of the inevitably higher turreted tanks.

PRE-PRODUCTION VEHICLES

The various features of the S-tank were extensively tested, starting in mid-1961 with one of the two prototypes. However, even before the manufacture of the first prototype was completed, the Swedish Army became so confident of the soundness of the S-tank concept that in mid-1960 it placed an order with Bofors for a pre-production series of ten vehicles. The first of these was completed in 1963 and they were subjected to further, much more extensive trials.

As was to be expected, the pre-production vehicles incorporated a number of changes called for by the testing of the prototypes and a number of features which the S-tank was intended to have from the beginning but which were left off the prototypes. One of the most obvious changes was the addition at the front of the hull of a stout bracket to support the gun tube, particularly against bending when it accidentally hit the ground. Following similar developments elsewhere, including

90

S-tank coming ashore with its flotation screen erected.

S-tank swimming with the aid of its flotation screen.

Pre-production model with the bulldozer blade locked in the working position; like the prototypes this vehicle has no track return rollers.

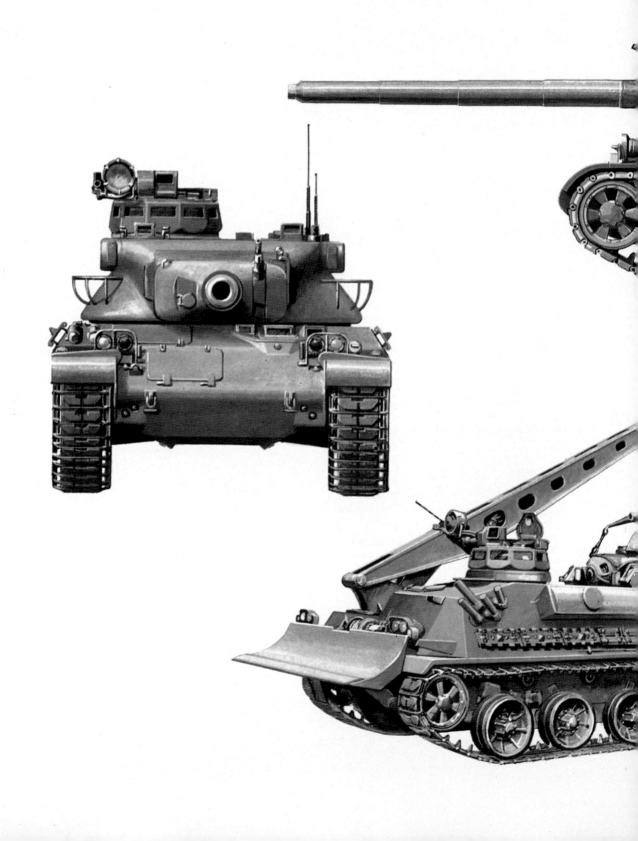

Top and left: Side and front views of AMX 30.

Below left: AMX 30D armoured recovery vehicle – *char AMX 30 depanneur-niveleur.*

Below right: the anti-aircraft tank – *AMX 30 bitube de 30mm.*

T. Hadler © Profile Publications Limited

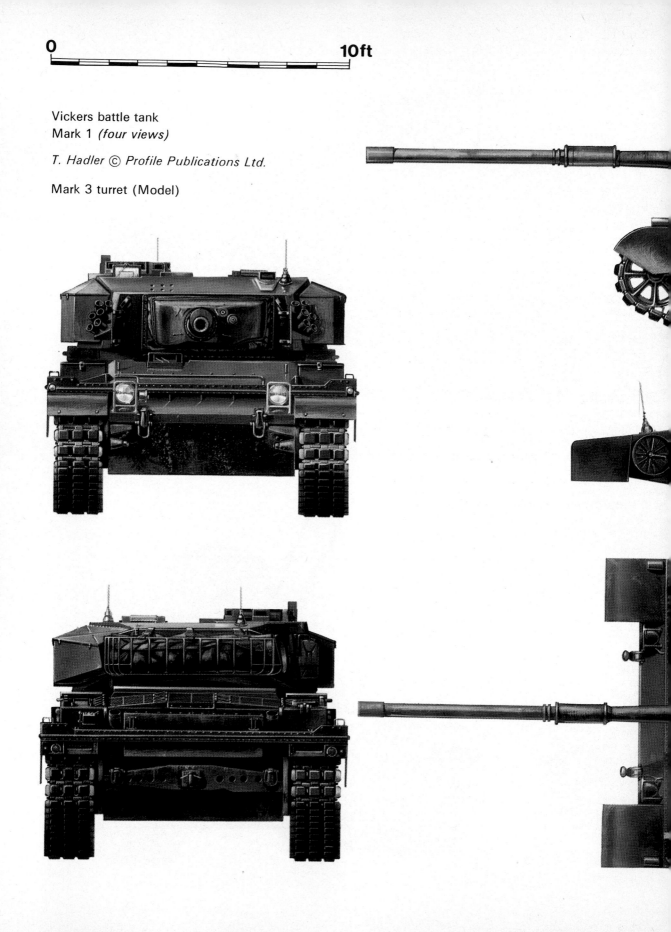

Vickers battle tank
Mark 1 *(four views)*

T. Hadler © Profile Publications Ltd.

Mark 3 turret (Model)

0
10ft

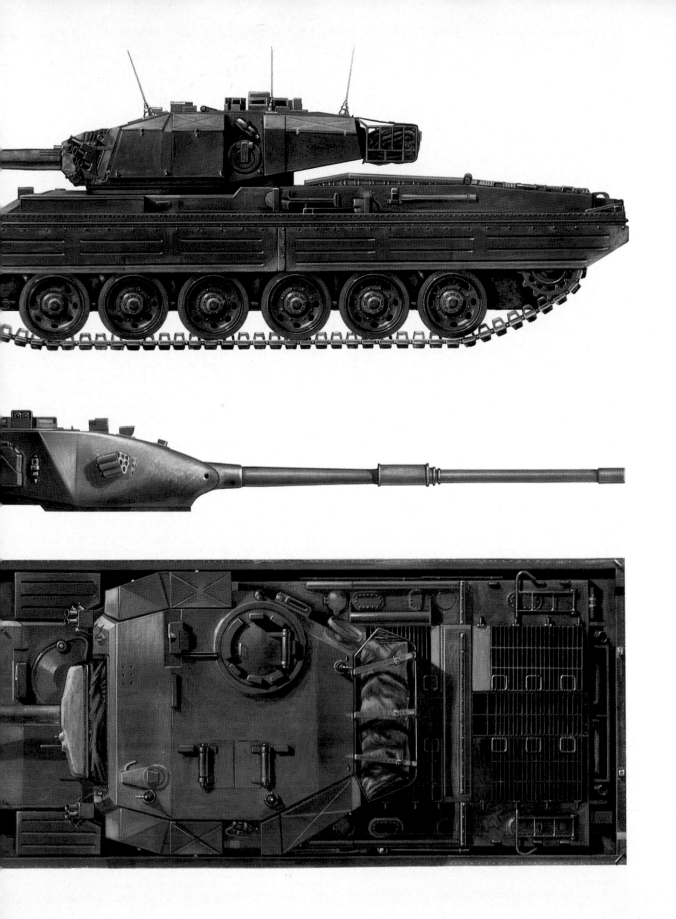

Beginning of the assembly of S-tanks at Bofors.

that of the British 105-mm. tank gun, the gun tube was also fitted with a fume extractor. This, together with the automatic ejection of spent cases outside the tank, virtually eliminated all chances of powder fumes entering the crew compartment.

Two return rollers were also added on each side to support the track which had previously rested on the tops of the road wheels and the track links had rubber pads bonded to them to improve road performance.

A less obvious change was the replacement of the right hand pair of 7.62-mm. machine-guns by a 12.7-mm. ranging machine-gun. The ranging machine-gun took the place of the optical range finder which was considered at first for the S-tank and which was fitted to most contemporary battle tanks, except in Britain where the 12.7-mm. ranging machine-gun was originally developed. However, the armoured boxes for the machine-guns were not fitted to all the pre-production vehicles and even when they were no weapon was generally fitted in the right-hand box because the idea of using a ranging machine-gun was abandoned by 1966.

Two other features of the S-tank which materialised only during the testing of the pre-production vehicles although they had been planned earlier were a collapsible flotation screen and a bulldozer blade. The flotation screen had been developed in Britain during the Second World War but the S-tank was the first battle tank designed to carry it permanently, neatly folded in a trough running round the upper part of the hull where it is protected from small arms bullets and shell fragments. The screen is slit at the front, to accomodate the protruding gun barrel, and when it is raised the slit is closed by means of clips. Altogether it takes the crew 15 minutes to erect the screen which enables the S-tank to float and paddle itself across inland water obstacles by means of its tracks at up to 5.5 km/hr. The propulsive effect of the tracks is increased by short shrouds fitted over their front part and the S-tank can enter or leave water at a more favourable attitude than other vehicles because the hull and the screen can be tilted by its adjustable suspension.

The adjustable suspension has also facilitated fitting

the S-tank with a bulldozer blade with which it can dig itself in for greater protection. Normally the blade is folded under the nose of the hull but when required it only needs to be swung forward and secured by means of two pin-ended tie-rods, which is done manually by the crew in about 5 minutes. Once this is done the vertical position of the blade and hence the depth of the cut is controlled by tilting the tank's hull by means of its suspension.

PRODUCTION MODEL

Testing of the pre-production vehicles and improving of the details of the design continued until 1967. Up to that time the cost of developing the S-tank, including the construction of the two prototypes and ten pre-production vehicles amounted to 120 million Swedish *kronor,* or £8.4 million at the contemporary rate of exchange. This meant that the development of the S-tank did not cost an undue amount and less in fact than that of several other tanks in spite of its novelty and sophistication.

In the meantime, the Swedish Army decided to adopt the S-tank for its armoured units and in July 1964 placed with Bofors a production order worth £33 million. The order began to bear fruit three years later when Bofors started to deliver the production model which they called S-tank Type A and which the Swedish Army designated Strv 103.

Externally the production models differed from the pre-production vehicles mainly in having ribbed armour, a new commander's cupola and stowage bins at the rear of the hull. However, their most interesting feature is the Jungner OPS–1 combination periscope and sight, one of which is provided for the commander and another for the driver/gunner. It consists of a unity magnification prismatic periscope with an exceptionally wide, 102 degree field of vision combined with a binocular sight whose magnification is six, ten or eighteen fold depending on the position of a small selector lever, and whose oculars are just below the bottom lens of the periscope. The driver/gunner's instrument is fixed but

Early production version of Strv 103, or S-tank Type A, without flotation equipment.

S-tank Type B with flotation equipment.

Rear view of an S-tank Type B with flotation equipment.

An S-tank with a mine exploding under one of its tracks during immunity trials; damage to the running gear could be repaired by the crew in about 3 hours.

the commander's is gyro-stabilised in elevation and mounted in a powered cupola which is gyro-stabilised in azimuth. In consequence the commander can observe on the move more easily that the commanders of other tanks and when he has acquired a target he can turn the tank to face it while retaining it in his sight.

On top of the commander's cupola is mounted a 7.62-mm. machine-gun which the commander can fire without exposing himself. In addition to the OPS-1 periscope/sight the commander's cupola also mounts four simple periscopes, instead of the American-type vision blocks of the original cupola, and there is also

one such periscope for the driver and two for the radio operator, which gives the crew complete, all-round vision. For the first time on any tank all periscopes are fitted with armoured visors which are operated by rods from within the tank. The visors not only provide protection against accidental damage when the periscopes are not in use but also can be used to eliminate reflections from the periscope glasses which prematurely give away the position of the tank at night.

The periscope/sight has also been developed to transmit laser pulses and echoes. Experiments with a laser range-finder for the S-tank started as early as

Contents of a napalm bomb burning around an S-tank which only required a few minutes' cleaning of optics to be fit for action again.

1965 and provision for installing it, coupled to the commander's or driver/gunner's periscope/sight, has been made in the production vehicles.

The original, Type A production model was fitted with the same gas turbine as the prototypes and pre-production vehicles but the later Type B has been fitted with the more powerful Boeing 553, produced in Belgium by F.N.-Boeing S.A., which was adopted in 1966. It develops 490 b.h.p. and has improved the performance of the tank, particularly its acceleration and average road speed.

TACTICAL PERFORMANCE

Delivery of the production vehicles enabled the S-tank to be tried on an increasingly large scale by the Swedish armoured units. The trials, which have been primarily of a tactical nature, confirmed that the S-tank can carry out all but one of the roles expected of battle tanks and that it has several advantages over turreted tanks. A similar

conclusion was reached in Britain where two S-tanks were evaluated in 1968.

The one thing which the S-tank can not do is to move in one direction and fire its main armament in another, as turreted tanks can. In other words, it can not engage major targets on the move, unless they happen to be at a short range straight ahead of it. This has given rise to much prejudice against it and the view, which obstinately persists in several quarters, that it is not a tank but only a limited-purpose tank destroyer.

However, all tanks have to stop to fire accurately, even when their guns are gyro-stabilised in elevation and azimuth. What really matters, therefore, is the relative speed with which the S-tank can stop and fire its gun, which depends on the overall reaction time. This is made up of a sequence of events whose duration has been significantly reduced in the S-tank or which have been entirely eliminated. In particular, because its commander and driver/gunner are both provided with a set of integrated driving and gun controls either can

Two S-tanks Type B passing through a Swedish village during winter manoeuvres.

An S-tank exposed to the shock wave of a simulated nuclear explosion.

stop the tank and fire its weapons by himself. Thus, the time which inevitably elapses in a conventional tank between the commander acquiring a target, issuing an order and the driver, gunner and loader acting on it has been eliminated. In consequence, the S-tank can react as quickly, or even quicker, than a conventional tank.

There are some occasions, of course, when the ability of the turreted tank to fire to either flank is an advantage, even though this implies having the relatively more vulnerable sides of the hull face the enemy. But in most other respects the S-tank has the advantage.

For instance, its possession of two engines reduces the chances of it being immobilised. Similarly, because the commander and driver/gunner are provided with duplicated driving and gun controls the S-tank can still be operated when either is incapacitated. In other words, in an emergency the S-tank can be effectively operated by one man. Under normal conditions the duplication of controls greatly reduces the strain on the crew. The configuration of the S-tank not only reduces the height of the target it presents but also facilitates the use of ground cover and, in particular, finding advantageous hull-down firing positions. It has also made it possible to provide its crew with a high degree of protection, in spite of the fact that at 37 tons the S-tank is one of the lightest members of the current generation of battle tanks.

The high degree of protection afforded by the S-tank was brought out particularly clearly during extensive immunity trials carried out between 1968 and 1970. During these trials S-tanks successfully survived the fire of high velocity tank guns, infantry anti-tank weapons and aircraft cannon, explosions of anti-tank mines, napalm bombs and even the blast of simulated nuclear explosions.

Summary of the Leading Characteristics of Strv 103 (S-tank Type B)

Gun, calibre	105-mm.
length	62 calibres
ammunition	50 rounds
Machine-guns, fixed	2 ×7.62-mm.
external	1 ×7.62-mm.
Weight, net	37000 kg
combat loaded	39000 kg
Length, with gun and stowage bins	9.8 m
without gun and bins	7.0 m
Width, overall	3.6 m
without removable fittings	3.4 m
Height, to roof over driver	1.9 m
to top of cupola	2.1 m
Ground clearance, at centre	0.5 m
at sides	0.4 m
Width of tracks	0.67 m
Track length to centre distance	1.1:1
Ground pressure	0.9 kg/cm²
Engine, diesel, make and model	Rolls-Royce K-60
gross horse power	240
gas turbine, make and model	FN-Boeing 553
gross horse power	490
Maximum road speed	50 km/hr
Range, on roads	300–400 km
Crew	3

Acknowledgements
The writer wishes to thank Mr. S. Berge for his help in retracing the history of the S-tank and Captain K. B. Jonell for other information about it. The writer also wishes to thank the Swedish Army Materiel Department and the Bofors Company for photographs and for making it possible for him to study the S-tank at different stages of its development.

Production version of the AMX 30 battle tank

AMX 30 Battle Tank

AT FIRST sight the AMX 30 looks like most other battle tanks of the 1960s and 1970s. On closer inspection, however, it proves to differ from its contemporaries in several important respects. In fact, its design embodies a number of novel ideas which make it one of the most interesting of modern battle tanks.

The attributes of the AMX 30 are in keeping with the distinguished record of the development of tanks in France. This goes back to the very first tanks, which were developed in France at the same time as in Britain, and over a period of nearly sixty years has produced many novel designs. It has also produced the term "battle tank", or *char de bataille,* which was first used in 1921 to describe one of two tanks the French Army intended to develop after the First World War, the other being a very heavy tank.

ORIGINAL CHAR DE BATAILLE

The heavy tank idea did not make much progress beyond the completion of ten 68-ton 2C tanks which were conceived before the end of the war in 1918. On the other hand the requirement for the *char de bataille,* which was re-defined in 1926, led to one of the most remarkable tanks ever built, the *char B*. This was a 31-ton vehicle armed with a 75mm gun which was mounted in the front of the hull so that it could be moved in elevation but not in azimuth in relation to the hull. In consequence, the gun was traversed on to a target by turning the whole vehicle which was done by the driver/gunner using a double-differential steering system with a hydrostatic steering drive.

The steering system and the semi-fixed gun mounting of the *char B* both represented remarkably advanced

design concepts. In fact, more than 30 years had to pass before other tanks were built with steering systems as sophisticated as that of the *char B*. As for the semi-fixed gun mounting, no other tank has yet been built with it, although there is now one tank with a completely fixed gun mounting, the S-tank developed in Sweden since 1956.

In some respects the *char B* was too far in advance of its day and it lacked some of the features which have made the S-tank so successful. In particular, it lacked the integrated driving and gun controls which make the S-tank so simple to operate. Thus, by the time it was produced in quantity in the 1930s, the *char B* was overtaken by other tanks so far as its overall effectiveness was concerned. To improve it, the semi-fixed mounting of the

Char B1 of the thirties, built to the original requirement for a char de bataille.

ARL 44, the transitional model built at the end of the Second World War.

75mm gun was abandoned, so that on the final *char B1 ter* version the gun could be not only elevated but also traversed, over an arc of 10 degrees, independently of the hull. The changes introduced in the *B1 ter* were not sufficient, however, to transform a brilliant concept into a really successful tank. Moreover, only five *chars B1 ter* were built before the French Army was defeated in 1940.

ARL 44

The occupation of France which followed the defeat of 1940 interrupted the development of French tanks. But clandestine studies continued under the German occupation and led to the design of a new battle tank which was built after the liberation of France in 1944. The new tank was called ARL 44 after the Atelier de Rueil and was first built in 1946. It weighed 48 tons and was powered by a 700 hp. engine which gave it a maximum road speed of 40 km./hour. Its main armament consisted of a turret-mounted 90mm gun capable of firing armour-piercing projectiles with a muzzle velocity of 1000 m/s. In all this the ARL 44 was comparable to other contemporary tanks but in other respects it was inferior to them. In fact, it retained several features of a design which was proposed in 1940 but which was never built, the ARL 40. For instance, its track layout, which resembled that of the *char B,* was distinctly old-fashioned by the standards of the late 1940s.

The ARL 44 could only be regarded, therefore, as a stop-gap vehicle, to be produced pending the development of another, thoroughly modern tank and it was, in fact, called a *char de transition.* Three hundred were originally ordered but in the end only 60 were built, which was just sufficient to equip one tank regiment, the 503rd. But, even as a temporary substitute, the ARL 44 did not prove entirely satisfactory and in the early 1950s it was withdrawn from service.

AMX 50

The stop-gap nature of the ARL 44 was emphasised by the fact that even before the first one was built work started on a much more modern and more powerful battle tank, the AMX 50. Work on the AMX 50 started as early as March 1945, that is two months before the end of the war in Europe. It was developed as part of the French Army's post-war re-equipment programme which called for only one battle tank in addition to two other armoured vehicles, an air-transportable light tank and a wheeled armoured reconnaissance vehicle. The French Army's policy of developing only one battle tank differed from the contemporary policies of the British, the United States and the Soviet Armies which continued to develop two categories of battle tanks, namely medium, or medium gun, and heavy, or heavy gun, tanks. It was, however, a sounder policy and proved to be so when, during the 1950s, the other armies also concentrated their efforts on a single type of battle tank.

The specification which led to the AMX 50 was strongly influenced by the characteristics of the two outstanding German tanks of the latter part of the Second World War, the Panther and the Tiger. Both these tanks were closely studied by French engineers who aimed at producing a tank which would be as mobile as the Panther and, at the same time, at least as well-armed as the Tiger. Thus, the AMX 50 was armed with guns of 90, 100 and finally 120mm and was powered by a 1000 hp. Maybach fuel-injection spark-ignition engine which grew out of a model intended for German tanks. The design of the AMX 50 also followed German tanks in such matters as the overlapping arrangement of its torsion bar sprung road wheels and in using a ZF gearbox similar to that of the Panther.

However, the AMX 50 also incorporated some highly original features. In particular, it had an oscillating, or trunnion-mounted, turret which had not been used before in any battle tank. This type of turret consisted of two parts, the upper part being mounted on trunnions in the lower part. The gun was fixed in the upper part and was elevated or depressed with it, which greatly simplified fire control equipment and the installation of an automatic loading mechanism, since there was no relative motion between them and the gun mounting.

The design of the AMX 50 was carried out at the Atelier de Construction d'Issy-les-Moulineaux, the French Army's armoured vehicle development centre, from whose initials and its target weight of 50 tons its designation was derived. The first was completed by the end of 1949. It was still armed with the same 90mm gun as the ARL 44, but by July 1950 another prototype was built armed with a 100mm gun. A second prototype with a 100mm gun was built shortly afterwards but in 1951 it was decided to abandon the 100mm gun in favour of an even more powerful 120mm gun. Thus, one of the three AMX 50 chassis was fitted with a new, larger turret mounting the 120mm gun, which had already been installed in a turretless, assault gun version of the AMX 50 built in prototype form in 1950.

Like the 90 and 100mm guns, designed by the Arsenal de Tarbes the 120mm gun developed by the Atelier du Havre fired conventional armour-piercing projectiles with a muzzle velocity of about 1000 m/s. Armed with it the AMX 50 became comparable to the contemporary

U.S. M103 (originally T43) and British Conqueror heavy tanks. It was, therefore, as powerful as any tank of its period and a production of about 100 was envisaged for 1956. However, the AMX50 was never put into production, mainly for financial reasons. An additional factor was a waning enthusiasm for very heavy tanks. This happened not only in France but also in Britain and in the United States where the Conqueror and the M103 were only produced in small quantities. Moreover, the French Army's immediate need for more modern tanks than the United States-built M4 mediums with which it was still equipped was met by the delivery of several hundred M47 medium tanks under the U.S. Military Aid Programme.

EUROPEAN TANK

When the AMX 50 was abandoned in the mid-1950s the French Army turned its attention to an entirely different type of battle tank, the AMX 30. This stemmed from a requirement arrived at in 1956 by the French General Staff in collaboration with the German and Italian Army Staffs. The joint Franco-German-Italian requirement was drawn up in an attempt to rationalize the development of weapons for the defence of Western Europe and called for a well-armed but lighter and more mobile type of battle tank than those which had been developed since the end of the Second World War in France, Britain and the United States. In fact, the new "European tank" was

Turretless version of the AMX 50 with a 120mm gun.

AMX 50 battle tank with a 100mm gun.

103

AMX 50 battle tank with a 120mm gun.

AMX 50 battle tank with a 120mm gun and a lowered hull.

Seventy-ton version of the AMX 50 with 120mm gun.

to weigh only 30 tons. This meant that it could not be heavily armoured. However, heavy armour was no longer considered to be as important as it had been because of the progress made in the development of anti-tank guided missiles and other weapons with shaped charge warheads which could perforate the thickest steel armour.

In addition to the relatively light weight of 30 tons the specification for the "European tank" agreed in 1957 by the French and German Armies called for a low silhouette and a high power-to-weight ratio, as well as a 105mm gun. From this basis the two armies proceeded in 1958 to design and then to construct prototypes from which a single European tank was to have been chosen, although in the event France and Germany each adopted its own design.

In France the design and development of the new battle tank was entrusted to the Atelier de Construction d'Issy-les-Moulineaux, which completed the first two prototypes of the AMX 30 in 1960. Seven more experimental tanks were built by the spring of 1963 and in July of that year the French government decided to put the AMX 30 into production for the French Army.

AMX 30 PROTOTYPES

The prototypes of the AMX 30 represented in many ways a striking contrast to their predecessor and to other contemporary tanks. To start with, the first two weighed only 32.5 tons, which made them lighter than any tank of comparable power. As well as being light they were also very compact. For instance, their overall width was only 3.1m, which could only be matched by one other battle tank, the Swiss Pz.61, and which implied easier transport by rail as it was within the international load gauge. What is more, the height of the AMX 30 was only 2.28m, measured to the turret roof. This is bettered by only one other turreted battle tank, namely the Soviet T-54 but at the expense of reducing the depression of its gun to only 4 degrees whereas the gun of the AMX 30 can be depressed

Batignolles experimental battle tank chassis which preceded the development of the AMX 30.

8 degrees, which is virtually the same as the maximum depression in other tanks.

In contrast to the AMX 50 and the other two vehicles of the previous generation, the AMX 13 and the Panhard EBR, the AMX 30 has been fitted with a conventional instead of an oscillating turret. The latter was found to suffer from several disadvantages which outweighed its advantages. In particular, it was very difficult to seal against radioactive dust or airborne chemical agents and against water during submerged crossing of rivers which the AMX 30 was expected to do. The oscillating type of turret also proved to be heavier and higher than conventional turrets and to provide less elevation for the gun mounted in it. In addition, it required a more powerful type of elevating gear and was potentially vulnerable to the jamming of its two parts. For all these reasons it was abandoned. It is worth noting that similar conclusions were reached elsewhere. Thus, following their successful introduction in French vehicles, oscillating turrets were incorporated in several United States tank designs, mainly because they facilitated the installation of automatic loading mechanisms. Experimental models of at least two of these tanks with oscillating turrets, the

Prototype of the AMX 30.

Pre-production version of the AMX 30: note absence of thermal sleeve on gun barrel.

Pre-production version of the AMX 30.

T54E1 and the T69, were actually built in the United States during the mid-1950s but none was ever put into production.

Unlike the earlier French armoured vehicles, the AMX 30 was also diesel powered. Prior to its development N.A.T.O. armies followed the policy that armoured vehicles should be powered by spark ignition engines, which were favoured after the Second World War because the demands of civilian peacetime economy made gasoline more readily available than diesel fuel in any emergency. As a result the prototypes of the AMX 30 were originally powered by a spark ignition engine, the SOFAM 12 GSds. This was a water-cooled, horizontally-opposed flat-twelve which developed 720 hp. In consequence the first two prototypes had a power-to-weight ratio of 22 hp. per ton, which was only exceeded several years later by the MBT-70, the experimental U.S.-German main battle tank.

However, by the time the AMX 30 began to be developed the N.A.T.O. armies finally recognised the advantages of using compression ignition engines in tanks. Thus, they abandoned their earlier policy but they did not adopt the obvious alternative of diesel engines. Instead they called for "multi-fuel engines". These were to operate on fuels ranging from diesel oil to gasoline, but they turned out to be diesels which are generally capable of operating on a wide range of fuels – given

some precautions whose elimination was the principal feature of the new generation of the so-called "multi-fuel" compression ignition tank engines.

Thus, in keeping with this change in policy, the development of the AMX 30 was accompanied by the development of a new, compression ignition engine. The new engine was developed by the Hispano-Suiza Diesel Division of S.N.E.C.M.A. and had the same output as the SOFAM spark ignition engine. At the same time it was not significantly different in size, which represented a considerable achievement because diesels have a lower specific output than spark ignition engines, and this made it possible to replace the earlier engines without undue difficulty. This was in fact done in the series of seven experimental tanks built by 1963, whose SOFAM engines were replaced by Hispano-Suiza engines.

GUN AND AMMUNITION

The most unusual feature of the AMX 30 from the start has been its main armament. This consists of a 105mm gun which fires a unique type of armour-piercing shaped charge projectile, the *Obus à Charge Creuse de 105mm Modèle F1,* or OCC 105 F1, often referred to as the *Obus G.*

The *Obus G* stems from a decision taken in 1953 by the Direction des Études et Fabrications d'Armement

Pre-production version of the AMX 30 during firing trials: circular port in side of turret allows ejection of spent cartridge cases.

Overhead view of a pre-production model showing the early type of louvres over the engine compartment.

(D.E.F.A., since known as the Direction Technique des Armements Terrestre, or D.T.A.T.) to develop a projectile for tank guns which would exploit to the full the armour-piercing capabilities of shaped charges. Its development faced the problem that shaped charges contained in conventional projectiles lose much of their armour-piercing performance because of the spin imparted to the projectiles by the rifling of the guns from which they are fired. The alternative, fin-stabilised projectiles spin little if at all but they have been considerably less accurate, particularly at long range. What was needed, therefore, was a projectile in which, as in fin-stabilised projectiles, the shaped charge would not spin to any significant extent but which would at the same time retain the accuracy of the spin-stabilised projectiles.

These apparently conflicting requirements were reconciled by the development of the *Obus G* in which the shaped charge is mounted in ball bearings. The outer body of the projectile can, therefore, be allowed to spin so that it retains a high degree of accuracy, but the shaped charge within it does not rotate at more than 20 to 30 revolutions per minute which does not degrade its performance.

In fact, the OCC 105 F1 can penetrate solid steel to a depth of 360 to 400mm, which is sufficient to perforate the armour of any contemporary battle tank. Moreover, its armour-piercing performance, like that of other shaped charge projectiles, is independent of range. This, together with its small dispersion and a muzzle velocity of 1,000 m/s makes it effective against tanks at up to 3,000 metres.

The development of a projectile as sophisticated as the OCC 105 F1 inevitably took several years but in 1961 a satisfactorily high level of performance had been reached for it to be accepted for use in the AMX 30. As expected, it has proved more accurate at long ranges than the equivalent type of fin-stabilised shaped charge, or HEAT (High Explosive Anti-Tank) projectile developed in the United States for 105mm tank guns. At the same time it is more versatile than solid armour-piercing shot and more difficult to defeat than squash head, or HESH, projectiles. In fact, it could have been used almost as the only type of tank gun projectile. It represented therefore almost the ideal tank gun ammunition, because the elimination of the variety of rounds which are carried in tanks would relieve tank crews of the need to select the appropriate type of round under the stress of battle and would thereby greatly increase the effectiveness of tanks.

However, because of its cost and specialised nature the OCC 105 F1 was inevitably less efficient against unarmoured targets than a more conventional high explosive shell. A complementary high explosive round was therefore also developed and so was a phosphorus smoke round as well as an illuminating round and a practice, dummy round. But in contrast to other tanks the AMX 30 has not been provided with armour-piercing discarding sabot rounds, both because they were considered unnecessary and because they require rifling with a greater degree of twist than that adopted to suit the OCC 105 F1.

TURRET ASSEMBLY

The service version of the AMX 30 crystallised in 1965 with the construction of two pre-production vehicles. These incorporated all the improvements introduced on the previous nine vehicles, as well as some additional

ones, and they were closely followed by production models the first of which was completed in June 1966.

Almost inevitably, the production version of the AMX 30 is heavier than the prototypes, although not to the same extent as some other tanks. In fact, it weighs 36 tons fully laden and it is still as light as any contemporary battle tank. Without its crew and ammunition it weighs 34 tons, of which approximately 10 is accounted for by the turret assembly.

The turret consists of a one-piece steel casting with well sloped sides which increase the effectiveness of its armour against attack by armour-piercing projectiles. In addition to the main armament of the 105mm gun there is alongside it a 12·7mm heavy machine-gun which is normally elevated with the gun up to a maximum of 20 degrees. However, there is provision for elevating it by itself another 20 degrees, that is giving it a maximum elevation of 40 degrees so that it can be used against helicopters as well as ground targets. There is also provision for replacing the 12·7mm machine-gun by a 20mm automatic cannon which would make the secondary armament of the AMX 30 even more effective. There is also a 7·62mm machine-gun mounted externally on the commander's cupola but aimed and fired from within it.

The commander's TOP 7 cupola offers exceptionally good all-round vision through a ring of 10 direct-vision periscopes and it also contains a x10 magnification binocular telescope for long range observation and target detection. The cupola is also provided with a counter-rotating mechanism so that the commander can bring the turret round to lay the gun on target without losing sight of it through unwanted rotation of the cupola. The commander also operates an optical range finder of the full-field coincidence or superposition type. This has a base of 2m and in addition to ranging can be used as a telescope to enable the commander to lay the gun by himself.

The gunner who, as in other tanks, sits in front of the commander, has a telescopic gun sight and two observation periscopes. Three more periscopes are provided for the loader/radio operator who occupies the left side of the turret. All this makes the AMX 30 exceptionally well provided with observation equipment and is in keeping with its high mobility. In fact, if it had not been as well provided with observation equipment as it is it could not have exploited its mobility to the full because the crew could not have observed well enough for it to move as fast as it can.

To improve its accuracy still further the 105mm gun is fitted with a magnesium alloy thermal sleeve which protects the 56 calibre long barrel from bending due to non-uniform cooling by side wind or heating by solar radiation. The gun can be fired at a rate of up to 8 rounds per minute and the ammunition supply for it consists of 50 rounds: 18 of these are in the turret bustle and four by the loader, the rest being stowed in the front of the hull, to the right of the driver.

The gun is elevated by means of a hydraulic jack and the turret traversed by a hydraulic motor which forms part of a control system developed for the Société d'Application des Machines Motrices (SAMM). Elevation and traverse are normally controlled by the gunner but the commander is provided with override controls so that he can, if necessary, fire the gun by himself. There is also a mechanical back-up system which can be used by the gunner.

Assembly line of AMX 30 turrets.

AUTOMOTIVE CHARACTERISTICS

The hull of the AMX 30 is welded from castings and
rolled plates and has an exceptionally well sloped glacis
which makes an angle of no less than 70 degrees with the
vertical. The sides of the hull underside are also sloped,
at 24 degrees to the horizontal, for improved protection
against mines.

As in other tanks, the rear portion of the hull is occupied by the engine and transmission assembly, which
can be replaced, if necessary, in 45 minutes. The engine
is the HS-110 diesel which was developed by Hispano-
Suiza but which is produced by SAVIEM, the heavy
vehicle division of the Renault organization. It is a very
compact, water-cooled engine with two horizontally-
opposed banks of six cylinders and two exhaust gas
turbine-driven superchargers. The twelve cylinders have
a total swept volume of 28·8 litres out of which the engine
develops 720 hp. at 2,600 revolutions per minute. In
consequence, the AMX 30 has a power-to-weight ratio
of 20 hp. per ton even when fully laden, and a maximum
road speed of 65 km./hr.

The engine is of the indirect-injection four stroke type
which makes it efficient over a wide speed range. This,
together with a total fuel tank capacity of 970 litres,
gives the AMX 30 a range of 500 to 600 km. on roads.
Under varying combat conditions, when for 20 per cent
of the time the tank may be assumed to operate on roads,
40 per cent off the roads, and for 40 per cent of the time
to be stationary but with the engine running, the fuel
is sufficient for 18 hours.

Close up of gun mantlet showing the coaxial 20mm gun elevated beyond
the maximum elevation of the 105mm gun.

TOP 7 commander's cupola on the production version of the AMX 30
battle tank.

The drive from the engine is taken through a Gravina twin-plate centrifugal clutch to an AMX gearbox. This provides 5 speeds forward and 5 in reverse and incorporates a triple differential steering system. Like other steering systems of this kind, that of the AMX 30 provides turning radii which vary with the propulsion gears, the lower the gear the smaller being the turning radius, which is generally required. Moreover, when the propulsion gears are in neutral the system causes the tracks to be driven in opposite directions so that the tank executes a pivot turn.

Each track of the AMX 30 consists of 83 steel links with plain steel connecting pins and detachable rubber road pads. The links are 570mm wide and in consequence the tracks exert a nominal pressure on the ground of only 0·77 kg./cm.², which is as low as that of any contemporary battle tank. Moreover, the tracks have a life of 5,000 km. or more, depending on the terrain, which again compares very favourably with that of the tracks of other battle tanks.

The weight of the AMX 30 is transferred to the tracks by double, medium-size, rubber-tyred road wheels of which there are five on each side. The wheels are sprung by transversely mounted torsion bars and located by arms, the second and fourth being trailing, and the first,

third and fifth leading. The location of the first, third and fifth wheels on leading arms differs from most other torsion bar suspensions where all arms are trailing and torsion bars are, in consequence, spread at equal intervals across the hull. This is less efficient, in terms of internal space, than the arrangement adopted in the AMX 30 which has helped to keep its silhouette low.

To help keep down the unsprung weight and also the total weight of the vehicle, the road wheels are of aluminium alloy. The first and fifth wheels on each side are fitted with hydraulic dampers and on each side there are also five small rubber-tyred rollers to support the top run of the track.

Another interesting feature of the AMX 30 is its ability to cross water obstacles. Not only can it ford water 1·3m deep without any preparation but with very little preparation it can operate in water up to 2m deep, that is with only the top of the turret showing above the surface, and after the fitting of a schnorkel tube to the loader's hatch it can operate completely submerged in water up to 4m deep. Apart from the fitting of the schnorkel tube and simple checks, virtually all that needs to be done to permit submerged operation is the installation of blanking plates, which are normally carried on the front of the hull, over the engine compartment air

Rear view of the production version of the AMX 30 battle tank.

Production version of the AMX 30 with a schnorkel tube for submerged fording.

AMX 30 moving under water with only the schnorkel tube and tip of gun barrel showing above the surface.

Assembly of an AMX 30 hull.

intake louvres. Then, just before entering the water, the crew have only to inflate the turret ring, mantlet and cupola seals by means of an electrically driven compressor and to disengage the drive to the engine cooling fan.

PRODUCTION

The final assembly of the AMX 30 has been carried out at the Atelier de Construction de Roanne. The town of Roanne where this plant of the D.T.A.T. is located is in the Massif Central, almost mid-way between the cities of Lyon and St. Etienne. The plant was built during the First World War to the plans of André Citroën for the production of artillery shells but since 1952 its activities have been concerned with armoured vehicles and before producing the AMX 30 it produced 1,900 vehicles of the AMX 13 series.

The original order for the AMX 30 placed in 1963 called for about 300 vehicles but it was planned from the outset to produce about 1,000 for the French Army alone and the eighth batch of 143 was in fact ordered in 1971. In addition to those built for the French Army, AMX 30 battle tanks have also been produced for the Greek Army, which adopted it to supplement its American-built tanks, and in 1972 the Venezuelan Army also ordered 142. Further AMX 30s have been ordered by the Spanish and Saudi Arabian Armies.

For export a somewhat simpler version has been offered as an alternative to the model produced for the French Army. This so-called "basic AMX 30" has a S.470 commander's cupola of the type originally fitted on the prototypes of the AMX 30, which is simpler and considerably lower than the TOP 7 cupola. To satisfy

users wedded to the bad traditions of United States tanks, the cupola carries an externally mounted 12·7mm machine-gun while the coaxial machine-gun is of 7·62mm calibre.

The "basic AMX 30" is also devoid of the infra-red searchlights and periscopes for observing and firing at night, and of the pressurised air filtering system for protection against radioactive dust and airborne biological or chemical agents. It also lacks a heater for the crew compartment but this, like the other equipment, can be fitted if required.

A considerably different version has been considered for future use by the French Army, namely one armed with a 142mm gun capable of firing ACRA guided missiles as well as high explosive projectiles. This would have given the French Army a tank somewhat similar but superior to the U.S. M60A2 battle tank armed with the 152mm gun/launcher. In particular, the ACRA missiles are supersonic infra-red beam riders and more advanced than the Shillelagh missiles fired from the U.S. 152mm gun/launcher. Moreover, both the ACRA missiles and the complementary high explosive rounds have conventional brass cartridge cases which means that they can be handled like conventional tank gun ammunition and are free of the problems which have bedevilled the U.S. 152mm gun/launchers with their combustible cartridge case rounds. However, for all its virtues, the development of the ACRA system was shelved in 1972 because of the inevitably high cost of its missiles.

In the meantime, several new features have been developed for the existing AMX 30 to improve its performance still further. These include stabilization of its 105mm gun in elevation and of the turret in azimuth

Basic model of the production version of the AMX 30.

Frontal view of the basic model of the AMX 30.

Production version of the AMX 30 with sand shields.

and, what is even more important, of a fire control system based on a laser range finder.

Several other vehicles have also been developed on the basis of the AMX 30. These include an armoured recovery vehicle, a bridgelayer, an anti-aircraft tank, a tactical nuclear missile launcher, and an experimental 155mm self-propelled gun.

RECOVERY VEHICLE

The AMX 30 D armoured recovery vehicle, or *char AMX 30 depanneur-niveleur*, has been developed to support AMX 30 battle tanks by towing any that might be disabled or pulling out of difficulties temporarily immobilised tanks, by replacing major assemblies, and by preparing passages for them, particularly during river-crossing operations. To enable it to do all this, the recovery vehicle has been fitted with a powerful winch, a crane and a bulldozer blade.

The winch is driven by the vehicle's engine through a torque converter and can exert a pull of up to 35 tons. Its heavy cable is 80m long and to haul it out there is an auxiliary winch which has a 120m long cable and can exert a maximum pull of 4 tons. The auxiliary winch can, of course, also be used whenever the nature of the recovery operation does not call for the main winch.

The crane is hydraulically operated and can lift loads of up to 13 tons over a sector of 240 degrees and 20 tons when working over the front of the vehicle: in the latter case it needs to be supported by removable props carried on the vehicle and the bulldozer blade needs to be lowered on to the ground to stabilise the vehicle. As a result, the recovery vehicle can not only lift a complete 3·29-ton engine and transmission assembly or the 10-ton turret assembly but it can even partly lift a complete AMX 30 tank.

The bulldozer blade, which is 3·14m wide, is also hydraulically operated and is used not only for earth-moving or excavating but also as a ground anchor when heavy loads are winched or, as already indicated, when the vehicle needs to be stabilized for lifting heavy loads.

Apart from its special equipment the recovery vehicle consists essentially of the AMX 30 battle tank chassis with a fixed superstructure instead of the gun turret. Its laden weight is normally the same as that of the battle tank, namely 36 tons, but when it carries a replacement engine-transmission assembly, for which there is a special frame above its own engine compartment, its weight reaches 40 tons.

The crew of the recovery vehicle consists of four men: commander, driver and two mechanics. The driver sits higher and further forward than in the battle tank and his compartment contains all the vehicle controls. The commander is located behind the driver and is provided with the same TOP 7 cupola as the commanders of battle tanks, which gives him excellent all-round vision, and a 7·62mm machine-gun for close-in defence of the vehicle. The two mechanics sit behind the commander.

The crew of the recovery vehicle are provided with the same nuclear, biological and chemical (NBC) protection as the crew of battle tanks and its automotive performance is virtually the same as that of the battle tanks. This means that it is highly mobile and when fitted with a schnorkel tube over the mechanics' hatch it can ford rivers submerged.

BRIDGELAYER

The AMX 30 bridgelayer, or *poseur de pont,* consists of a standard battle tank chassis with a box-like superstructure instead of the gun turret, supports for carrying a scissors-type folding bridge, and a hydraulically operated mechanism for laying and retrieving the bridge over the rear of the vehicle. When unfolded the bridge is 22m long, which enables it to span gaps 20m or, when the banks are hard, 21m wide. The width of the bridge is

Armoured recovery version of the AMX 30.

AMX 30 recovery vehicle with its crane raised to lift an engine and transmission assembly.

AMX 30 bridgelayer with bridge in travelling position.

AMX 30 anti-aircraft tank.

AMX 30 with S 401 A turret mounting two 30mm automatic guns and fire control radar.

3·10m but this can be increased to 3·95m by the use of additional panels.

The bridge has a class 50 rating which means that it can normally carry tracked vehicles of up to 40 tons and with special care of up to 46 tons. It can also carry wheeled vehicles with a load per axle of 16 tons. The bridge itself weighs 7·25 tons. Widening panels and central flooring panels weigh another 1·35 tons and bring the weight of the bridgelayer with the bridge to 42·6 tons.

The bridgelayer is manned by a crew of three, those additional to the driver being the commander and the bridge operator both of whom are located in the super-structure. The operator controls the laying and recovery of the bridge by himself and either operation can be accomplished in about 10 minutes. If necessary this can be done with all the hatches closed and as the bridge-layer is provided with NBC equipment similar to that of the battle tanks it can be used to lay bridges even in contaminated areas.

Apart from being heavier as well as 4·29m high and 11·5m long, when carrying the bridge, the bridgelayer has much the same performance as the AMX 30 battle tank from which it was derived and it can, therefore, operate over the same type of terrain.

ANTI-AIRCRAFT TANK

Development of the turret assembly of the AMX 30 anti-aircraft tank which gives it its special characteristics antedates that of the AMX 30 battle tanks. This is due to the foresight of the French Army which, like the Soviet Army, continued to develop self-propelled anti-aircraft guns for defence against low-level attacks at the time when other armies had unwisely neglected them. Its development was focussed on twin Hispano-Suiza 30mm 831 A automatic guns coupled to an *Oeil-noir* fire control radar which were installed in a SAMM S 401 A turret and this was mounted on an AMX 13 light tank chassis – the only suitable armoured vehicle chassis available to the French Army at the time.

The combination of the S 401 A turret with the AMX 13 chassis represented a significant advance on all earlier self-propelled anti-aircraft guns and in March 1962 the French General Staff decided to put it into production. Quantity production actually began in 1967 and the AMX 13 anti-aircraft tank came into service as the *Bitube de 30mm Anti-aerien Automoteur*.

However, production of the AMX 30 provided another chassis on which the S 401 A turret could be mounted and this resulted in an even better mobile anti-aircraft weapon system. To start with, the automotive charac-teristics of the AMX 30 chassis are greatly superior to those of the AMX 13. As it is twice as heavy as the AMX 13, the AMX 30 also provides a much more stable platform for the guns. Most important of all, perhaps, the AMX 30 can carry much more ammunition: 1,200 rounds, in fact, which is twice the number of rounds carried by the AMX 13 anti-aircraft tank.

The guns are normally used to fire bursts of one, 5 or 15 rounds each, at a cyclic rate of fire of 650 rounds per minute per gun. They are controlled by an electronic analogue computer from the basis of information about the range of the target fed by a Doppler radar and about the motion of the target provided by the gunner visually tracking it. Prior to being used for determining the range of the target, the radar is used for surveillance and for detecting the direction of the target, the second phase of the target acquisition being optical. When not in use the radar aerial can be neatly folded down into an armoured box at the back of the turret to protect it from accidental damage. This also reduces the overall height of the vehicle from 3·8m to 3m.

As it depends on visual tracking, the fire control system is only of the "clear weather" type but adequate, nevertheless, for dealing with the most likely form of low level aerial attack and is very much simpler and less expensive than any alternative "all-weather" system. The crew of the *AMX 30 bitube de 30 mm* consists of only three men. They are the commander who controls the first phase of target acquisition, and the gunner, who controls the second phase and fires the guns, both of whom sit in the turret, and the driver. The chassis differs from that of the other vehicles of the series in housing a small generator set which makes it possible to operate the turret without running the main engine.

MISSILE LAUNCHER

In addition to having a better appreciation than most other armies of the importance of anti-aircraft tanks, the French Army has also recognised the need for suitable mobile launchers for tactical nuclear missiles, in contrast to the U.S. Army and others equipped with American tactical missiles. The only army which has been ahead of the French in this respect is the Soviet Army which has developed a series of tracked missile launchers based on tank chassis.

The French Army's answer to the need for a mobile tactical missile launcher has been, once again, to choose the chassis of the AMX 30 and to modify it to carry the container/launching ramp of the Pluton surface-to-surface tactical nuclear missile. The missile weighs 2·4 tons and is 7·6m long; it has a simplified inertial guidance system and a solid propellant rocket motor which gives it

Service version of the AMX 30 Pluton missile launcher.

Prototype of the AMX 30 Pluton tactical nuclear missile launcher.

a maximum range of 120 km., while its minimum range is 10 km. It can be fired with a minimum of preparation and the vehicle on which it is mounted has the same mobility as the AMX 30 battle tanks. The launcher, or *vehicule de tir Pluton*, can operate therefore in close support of armoured units. To help it in this the four-man crew of the AMX 30 Pluton launcher are provided with the same type of NBC protection as the crew of AMX 30 battle tanks.

SELF-PROPELLED GUN

Powerful as they are, Pluton and similar nuclear missiles have not eliminated the need for more conventional artillery support. In consequence yet another weapon system has been developed on the basis of the AMX 30. This is the *canon automoteur de 155 GCT*, a 155mm gun mounted in a special large turret on a standard AMX 30 battle tank chassis. The gun is 40 calibres long and is provided with an automatic loading mechanism which enables it to fire at a rate of 8 rounds per minute to a maximum range of 23·5 km.

The turret in which the 155mm gun is mounted has all-round traverse and allows the gun to be elevated up to 66 degrees. Ammunition carried in the vehicle for the gun consists of 42 rounds with combustible cartridge cases and fully laden it weighs 38 tons. Its crew consists of four men, three of whom are located in the turret and all of whom are provided with the same type of NBC protection as the crews of the other vehicles of the series. In several other respects the 155mm self-propelled gun also resembles the other vehicles of the AMX 30 family.

SUMMARY OF THE LEADING CHARACTERISTICS OF THE AMX 30 BATTLE TANK

Gun, calibre	105mm
length	56 calibres
ammunition	50 rounds
Machine-gun, coaxial	12·7mm
external	7·62mm
Weight, net (in travel order)	34,000 kg.
combat loaded	36,000 kg.
Length, overall, gun forward	9·48m
vehicle only	6·59m
Height, to turret roof	2·28m
to top of cupola telescope	2·85m
Width, overall	3·10m
Ground clearance	0·44m
Width of tracks	0·57m
Nominal ground pressure	0·77 kg./cm.²
Engine, model	HS 110
gross horse power	720
Maximum road speed	65 km./hr.
Range, on roads	500–600 km.
Crew	4

Acknowledgements

The author wishes to thank the Directors of the Atelier de Construction d'Issy-les-Moulineaux for information about the history and characteristics of the AMX 30 and for making it possible for him to examine it, on more than one occasion.

The author also wishes to thank the Directors of the Atelier de Construction d'Issy-les-Moulineaux, the Technical Director of the Direction Technique des Armements Terrestre and the Military Attachés at the French Embassy in London for their generous help with photographs.

All photographs are French Army copyright.

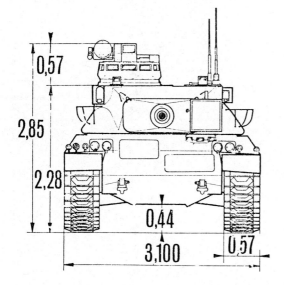

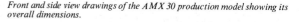

Front and side view drawings of the AMX 30 production model showing its overall dimensions.

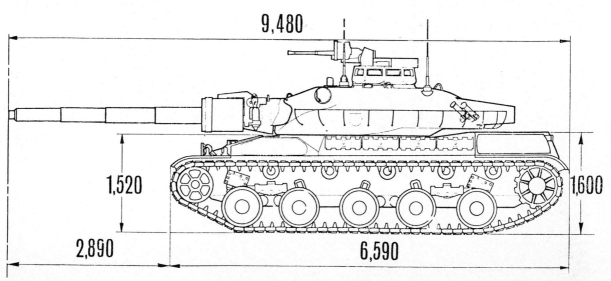